Working Papers

Chapters 14-26

Accounting 24e
or
Accounting Using Excel for Success 2e

Carl S. Warren
Professor Emeritus of Accounting
University of Georgia, Athens

James M. Reeve
Professor Emeritus of Accounting
University of Tennessee, Knoxville

Jonathan E. Duchac
Professor of Accounting
Wake Forest University

SOUTH-WESTERN
CENGAGE Learning

Australia • Brazil • Japan • Korea • Mexico • Singapore • Spain • United Kingdom • United States

© 2012 Cengage Learning. All Rights Reserved. May not be scanned, copied or duplicated, or posted to a publicly accessible website, in whole or in part.

© 2012, 2009 South-Western, Cengage Learning

ALL RIGHTS RESERVED. No part of this work covered by the copyright herein may be reproduced, transmitted, stored, or used in any form or by any means graphic, electronic, or mechanical, including but not limited to photocopying, recording, scanning, digitizing, taping, Web distribution, information networks, or information storage and retrieval systems, except as permitted under Section 107 or 108 of the 1976 United States Copyright Act, without the prior written permission of the publisher except as may be permitted by the license terms below.

For product information and technology assistance, contact us at
**Cengage Learning Academic Resource Center,
1-800-423-0563.**

For permission to use material from this text or product, submit all requests online at **www.cengage.com/permissions**.
Further permissions questions can be emailed to **permissionrequest@cengage.com**.

ISBN-13: 978-0-538-47854-0
ISBN-10: 0-538-47854-3

South-Western Cengage Learning
5191 Natorp Boulevard
Mason, OH 45040
USA

Cengage Learning is a leading provider of customized learning solutions with office locations around the globe, including Singapore, the United Kingdom, Australia, Mexico, Brazil, and Japan. Locate your local office at: **international.cengage.com/region**.

Cengage Learning products are represented in Canada by Nelson Education, Ltd.

For your course and learning solutions, visit **www.cengage.com**.

Purchase any of our products at your local college store or at our preferred online store **www.CengageBrain.com**.

NOTE: UNDER NO CIRCUMSTANCES MAY THIS MATERIAL OR ANY PORTION THEREOF BE SOLD, LICENSED, AUCTIONED, OR OTHERWISE REDISTRIBUTED EXCEPT AS MAY BE PERMITTED BY THE LICENSE TERMS HEREIN.

READ IMPORTANT LICENSE INFORMATION

Dear Professor or Other Supplement Recipient:

Cengage Learning has provided you with this product (the "Supplement") for your review and, to the extent that you adopt the associated textbook for use in connection with your course (the "Course"), you and your students who purchase the textbook may use the Supplement as described below. Cengage Learning has established these use limitations in response to concerns raised by authors, professors, and other users regarding the pedagogical problems stemming from unlimited distribution of Supplements.

Cengage Learning hereby grants you a nontransferable license to use the Supplement in connection with the Course, subject to the following conditions. The Supplement is for your personal, noncommercial use only and may not be reproduced, posted electronically or distributed, except that portions of the Supplement may be provided to your students IN PRINT FORM ONLY in connection with your instruction of the Course, so long as such students are advised that they may not copy or distribute any portion of the Supplement to any third party. Test banks and other testing materials may be made available in the classroom and collected at the end of each class session, or posted electronically as described herein. Any material posted electronically must be through a password-protected site, with all copy and download functionality disabled, and accessible solely by your students who have purchased the associated textbook for the Course. You may not sell, license, auction, or otherwise redistribute the Supplement in any form. We ask that you take reasonable steps to protect the Supplement from unauthorized use, reproduction, or distribution. Your use of the Supplement indicates your acceptance of the conditions set forth in this Agreement. If you do not accept these conditions, you must return the Supplement unused within 30 days of receipt.

All rights (including without limitation, copyrights, patents, and trade secrets) in the Supplement are and will remain the sole and exclusive property of Cengage Learning and/or its licensors. The Supplement is furnished by Cengage Learning on an "as is" basis without any warranties, express or implied. This Agreement will be governed by and construed pursuant to the laws of the State of New York, without regard to such State's conflict of law rules.

Thank you for your assistance in helping to safeguard the integrity of the content contained in this Supplement. We trust you find the Supplement a useful teaching tool.

Printed in the United States of America
1 2 3 4 5 6 7   14 13 12 11 10

CONTENTS

14	Long-Term Liabilities: Bonds and Notes	565
15	Investments and Fair Value Accounting	593
16	Statement of Cash Flows	637
17	Financial Statement Analysis	669
18	Managerial Accounting Concepts and Principles	709
19	Job Order Costing	729
20	Process Cost Systems	755
21	Cost Behavior and Cost-Volume-Profit Analysis	803
22	Budgeting	837
23	Performance Evaluation Using Variances from Standard Costs	871
24	Performance Evaluation for Decentralized Operations	911
25	Differential Analysis, Product Pricing, and Activity-Based Costing	941
26	Capital Investment Analysis	977

PREFACE

The working papers include problem-specific forms for preparing solutions for Exercises, A&B Problems, the Continuing Problem, and the Comprehensive Problems from the textbook. These forms, with preprinted headings, provide a structure for the problems, which will help you get started and save you time.

Based on students' testimonials and instructors' feedback, the forms in the working papers have been streamlined to make them simpler to use and to better reflect the changing environment of business. For example, the vertical rules that separated digits of numbers entered into journals, ledgers, and statements have been removed, making it easier to write in numbers. Also, the formats of the end-of-period spreadsheet (work sheet) and several other forms have been updated to better resemble actual electronic spreadsheets.

Note that when entering whole amounts into the forms, your instructor will direct you on whether to include a decimal point and zeroes (e.g., 100.00) or to omit those (e.g., 100).

Name _____   Chapter 14

EXERCISE 14-1

	a.	b.	c.
Earnings before bond interest and income tax			
Bond interest			
Balance			
Income tax			
Net income			
Dividends on preferred stock			
Earnings available for common stock			
Earnings per share on common stock			

EXERCISE 14-2

EXERCISE 14-3

EXERCISE 14-4

EXERCISE 14-5

JOURNAL   PAGE

	DATE	DESCRIPTION	POST. REF.	DEBIT	CREDIT	
1						1
2						2
3						3
4						4
5						5
6						6
7						7
8						8
9						9
10						10

Chapter 14 567

EXERCISE 14-6

a. 1. through 4.

JOURNAL   PAGE

	DATE	DESCRIPTION	POST. REF.	DEBIT	CREDIT	
1						1
2						2
3						3
4						4
5						5
6						6
7						7
8						8
9						9
10						10
11						11
12						12
13						13

b.

c.

EXERCISE 14-7

a. and b.

JOURNAL

PAGE

	DATE	DESCRIPTION	POST. REF.	DEBIT	CREDIT	
1						1
2						2
3						3
4						4
5						5
6						6
7						7
8						8
9						9
10						10

c.

EXERCISE 14-8

JOURNAL   PAGE

	DATE	DESCRIPTION	POST. REF.	DEBIT	CREDIT	
1						1
2						2
3						3
4						4
5						5
6						6
7						7
8						8
9						9
10						10
11						11
12						12
13						13

EXERCISE 14-9

JOURNAL   PAGE

	DATE	DESCRIPTION	POST. REF.	DEBIT	CREDIT	
1						1
2						2
3						3
4						4
5						5
6						6
7						7
8						8
9						9
10						10
11						11
12						12
13						13

570 Name _____ *Chapter 14*

EXERCISE 14-10

a. 1. and 2.

JOURNAL PAGE

	DATE	DESCRIPTION	POST. REF.	DEBIT	CREDIT	
1						1
2						2
3						3
4						4
5						5
6						6
7						7
8						8
9						9
10						10

b. _____

_____

_____

_____

Current Liabilities:		
Noncurrent Liabilities:		

EXERCISE 14-11

	DATE	DESCRIPTION	POST. REF.	DEBIT	CREDIT	
1						1
2						2
3						3
4						4
5						5
6						6
7						7
8						8
9						9
10						10
11						11
12						12
13						13
14						14
15						15
16						16
17						17
18						18

EXERCISE 14-12

a.

	Amortization of Installment Notes				
	A	**B**	**C**	**D**	**E**
For the Year Ending	**January 1 Carrying Amount**	**Note Payment (Cash Paid)**	**Interest Expense (9% of January 1 Note Carrying Amount)**	**Decrease in Notes Payable (B – C)**	**December 31 Carrying Amount (A – D)**

b.

JOURNAL

	DATE	DESCRIPTION	POST. REF.	DEBIT	CREDIT
1					
2					
3					
4					
5					
6					
7					
8					
9					
10					
11					
12					
13					
14					
15					
16					
17					

Name _____   Chapter 14 573

EXERCISE 14-12, Concluded

JOURNAL   PAGE

	DATE	DESCRIPTION	POST. REF.	DEBIT	CREDIT	
1						1
2						2
3						3
4						4
5						5
6						6
7						7
8						8
9						9
10						10
11						11
12						12
13						13

c. _____

_____

EXERCISE 14-13

1. _____

_____

_____

_____

2. _____

_____

_____

_____

_____

© 2012 Cengage Learning. All Rights Reserved. May not be scanned, copied or duplicated, or posted to a publicly accessible website, in whole or in part.

EXERCISE 14-14

a. _____

_____

_____

_____

_____

b. _____

EXERCISE 14-15

a. _____

_____

_____

_____

_____

b. _____

EXERCISE 14-16

a. _____

_____

_____

_____

_____

b. _____

APPENDIX 1 EXERCISE 14-17

_____

_____

_____

_____

_____

APPENDIX 1 EXERCISE 14-18

a.

b. _____

c. _____

APPENDIX 1 EXERCISE 14-19

APPENDIX 1 EXERCISE 14-20

APPENDIX 1 EXERCISE 14-21

APPENDIX 1 EXERCISE 14-22

Name _____   Chapter 14

APPENDIX 2 EXERCISE 14-23

a.

JOURNAL   PAGE

	DATE	DESCRIPTION	POST. REF.	DEBIT	CREDIT	
1						1
2						2
3						3
4						4
5						5
6						6
7						7
8						8
9						9
10						10
11						11
12						12
13						13
14						14
15						15

b.

c.

Name _____   *Chapter 14*

APPENDIX 2 EXERCISE 14-24

a.

JOURNAL   PAGE

DATE	DESCRIPTION	POST. REF.	DEBIT	CREDIT

b.

c.

APPENDIX 2 EXERCISE 14-25

a. through d.

APPENDIX 2 EXERCISE 14-26

a. through d.

Chapter 14

PROBLEM 14-1 ___

1.

	Plan 1	Plan 2	Plan 3
Earnings before interest and income tax			
Deduct interest on bonds			
Income before income tax			
Deduct income tax			
Net income			
Dividends on preferred stock			
Available for dividends on common stock			
Shares of common stock outstanding			
Earnings per share on common stock			

2.

	Plan 1	Plan 2	Plan 3
Earnings before interest and income tax			
Deduct interest on bonds			
Income before income tax			
Deduct income tax			
Net income			
Dividends on preferred stock			
Available for dividends on common stock			
Shares of common stock outstanding			
Earnings per share on common stock			

PROBLEM 14-1 ___, Concluded

3.

PROBLEM 14-2 ___

1. and 2.

JOURNAL

PAGE

	DATE	DESCRIPTION	POST. REF.	DEBIT	CREDIT	

3.

PROBLEM 14-2 ___, Concluded

4.

5.

Name _____   Chapter 14 585

PROBLEM 14-3 ___

1. and 2.

JOURNAL   PAGE

#	DATE	DESCRIPTION	POST. REF.	DEBIT	CREDIT	#
1						1
2						2
3						3
4						4
5						5
6						6
7						7
8						8
9						9
10						10
11						11
12						12
13						13
14						14
15						15
16						16
17						17
18						18
19						19
20						20
21						21
22						22
23						23
24						24
25						25

3.

PROBLEM 14-3 ___, Concluded

4.

5.

PROBLEM 14-4 ___

1.

JOURNAL

PAGE ___

	DATE	DESCRIPTION	POST. REF.	DEBIT	CREDIT	
1						1
2						2
3						3
4						4
5						5
6						6
7						7
8						8
9						9
10						10
11						11
12						12
13						13
14						14
15						15
16						16
17						17
18						18
19						19
20						20
21						21
22						22
23						23
24						24
25						25
26						26
27						27
28						28
29						29
30						30
31						31
32						32
33						33
34						34
35						35
36						36

Name _____   Chapter 14

PROBLEM 14-4 ___, Concluded

JOURNAL   PAGE

	DATE	DESCRIPTION	POST. REF.	DEBIT	CREDIT	
1						1
2						2
3						3
4						4
5						5
6						6
7						7
8						8
9						9
10						10
11						11
12						12
13						13
14						14
15						15

2. (a) 2012: _____

  (b) 2013: _____

3.

APPENDIX 2 PROBLEM 14-5 ___

1. and 2.

JOURNAL

PAGE _____

	DATE	DESCRIPTION	POST. REF.	DEBIT	CREDIT	
1						1
2						2
3						3
4						4
5						5
6						6
7						7
8						8
9						9
10						10
11						11
12						12
13						13
14						14
15						15
16						16
17						17
18						18
19						19

3.

_____

_____

_____

This Page Not Used.

Name _____ Chapter 14

APPENDIX 2 PROBLEM 14-6 ___

1. and 2.

JOURNAL   PAGE

	DATE	DESCRIPTION	POST. REF.	DEBIT	CREDIT	
1						1
2						2
3						3
4						4
5						5
6						6
7						7
8						8
9						9
10						10
11						11
12						12
13						13
14						14
15						15
16						16
17						17
18						18
19						19

3.

_____

_____

_____

_____

_____

_____

This Page Not Used.

EXERCISE 15-1

a. through d.

JOURNAL PAGE

	DATE	DESCRIPTION	POST. REF.	DEBIT	CREDIT	
1						1
2						2
3						3
4						4
5						5
6						6
7						7
8						8
9						9
10						10
11						11
12						12
13						13
14						14
15						15
16						16
17						17
18						18
19						19
20						20
21						21
22						22

Name _____

EXERCISE 15-2

a. through d.

JOURNAL   PAGE

	DATE	DESCRIPTION	POST. REF.	DEBIT	CREDIT	
1						1
2						2
3						3
4						4
5						5
6						6
7						7
8						8
9						9
10						10
11						11
12						12
13						13
14						14
15						15
16						16
17						17
18						18
19						19
20						20
21						21
22						22
23						23
24						24
25						25
26						26
27						27
28						28
29						29
30						30
31						31
32						32
33						33
34						34
35						35
36						36

EXERCISE 15-3

a. through d.

JOURNAL

PAGE

	DATE	DESCRIPTION	POST. REF.	DEBIT	CREDIT	
1						1
2						2
3						3
4						4
5						5
6						6
7						7
8						8
9						9
10						10
11						11
12						12
13						13
14						14
15						15
16						16
17						17
18						18
19						19
20						20
21						21
22						22
23						23
24						24
25						25
26						26
27						27
28						28
29						29
30						30
31						31
32						32
33						33
34						34
35						35
36						36

EXERCISE 15-4

a. and b.

JOURNAL PAGE

	DATE	DESCRIPTION	POST. REF.	DEBIT	CREDIT	
1						1
2						2
3						3
4						4
5						5
6						6
7						7
8						8
9						9
10						10
11						11
12						12
13						13
14						14
15						15
16						16
17						17
18						18
19						19
20						20
21						21
22						22
23						23
24						24
25						25

EXERCISE 15-5

EXERCISE 15-6

a., b., and c.

JOURNAL   PAGE

	DATE	DESCRIPTION	POST. REF.	DEBIT	CREDIT	
1						1
2						2
3						3
4						4
5						5
6						6
7						7
8						8
9						9
10						10
11						11
12						12
13						13
14						14
15						15

EXERCISE 15-7

JOURNAL   PAGE

	DATE	DESCRIPTION	POST. REF.	DEBIT	CREDIT	
1						1
2						2
3						3
4						4
5						5
6						6
7						7
8						8
9						9
10						10
11						11
12						12
13						13
14						14
15						15

EXERCISE 15-8

JOURNAL   PAGE

	DATE	DESCRIPTION	POST. REF.	DEBIT	CREDIT	
1						1
2						2
3						3
4						4
5						5
6						6
7						7
8						8
9						9
10						10
11						11
12						12
13						13
14						14
15						15
16						16
17						17
18						18
19						19
20						20
21						21
22						22
23						23
24						24

EXERCISE 15-9

JOURNAL

PAGE

	DATE	DESCRIPTION	POST. REF.	DEBIT	CREDIT	
1						1
2						2
3						3
4						4
5						5
6						6
7						7
8						8
9						9
10						10
11						11
12						12
13						13
14						14
15						15
16						16
17						17
18						18
19						19
20						20
21						21
22						22
23						23
24						24

EXERCISE 15-10

a. and b.

JOURNAL PAGE

	DATE	DESCRIPTION	POST. REF.	DEBIT	CREDIT	
1						1
2						2
3						3
4						4
5						5
6						6
7						7
8						8
9						9

c.

_____

_____

_____

EXERCISE 15-11

a.

JOURNAL PAGE

	DATE	DESCRIPTION	POST. REF.	DEBIT	CREDIT	
1						1
2						2
3						3
4						4
5						5
6						6
7						7
8						8
9						9
10						10
11						11
12						12
13						13
14						14

EXERCISE 15-11, Concluded

b.

EXERCISE 15-12

a.

JOURNAL

PAGE

	DATE	DESCRIPTION	POST. REF.	DEBIT	CREDIT
1					
2					
3					
4					
5					
6					
7					
8					
9					
10					
11					
12					
13					
14					

b.

EXERCISE 15-12, Concluded

c.

EXERCISE 15-13

EXERCISE 15-14

KVS Capital, Inc.
Selected Income Statement Items
For the Years Ended December 31, 2012 and 2013

	2012	2013
Operating income	a. _____	e. _____
Unrealized gain (loss)	b. _____	$ (3,000)
Net income	c. _____	19,000

Lydell Capital, Inc.
Selected Balance Sheet Items
December 31, 2011, 2012, and 2013

	Dec. 31, 2011	Dec. 31, 2012	Dec. 31, 2013
Trading investments, at cost	$123,000	$146,000	$172,000
Valuation allowance for investments	(4,000)	9,000	g. _____
Trading investments, at fair value	d. _____	f. _____	h. _____
Retained earnings	$156,000	$192,000	i. _____

EXERCISE 15-15

a.

JOURNAL

	DATE	DESCRIPTION	POST. REF.	DEBIT	CREDIT
1					
2					
3					
4					
5					
6					
7					
8					
9					
10					
11					
12					
13					
14					
15					
16					

b.

Name _____ Chapter 15 605

EXERCISE 15-16

a. and b.

JOURNAL PAGE

	DATE	DESCRIPTION	POST. REF.	DEBIT	CREDIT	
1						1
2						2
3						3
4						4
5						5
6						6
7						7
8						8
9						9
10						10
11						11
12						12
13						13
14						14
15						15
16						16
17						17
18						18
19						19
20						20

EXERCISE 15-17

a.

JOURNAL PAGE

	DATE	DESCRIPTION	POST. REF.	DEBIT	CREDIT	
1						1
2						2
3						3
4						4
5						5
6						6
7						7

Computations:

b. _____

EXERCISE 15-18

a.

b.

Name _____   Chapter 15   607

EXERCISE 15-19

Oceanic Airways
Selected Income Statement Items
For the Years Ended December 31, 2012 and 2013

	2010	2011
Operating income	a. _____	g. _____
Gain (loss) from sale of investments	$4,000	$ (8,000)
Net income	b. _____	(15,000)

Oceanic Airways
Selected Balance Sheet Items
December 31, 2011, 2012, and 2013

	Dec. 31, 2009	Dec. 31, 2010	Dec. 31, 2011
Assets			
Available-for-sale investments, at cost	$ 78,000	$ 68,000	$95,000
Valuation allowance for available-for-sale investments	6,000	(9,000)	h. _____
Available-for-sale investments, at fair value	c. _____	e. _____	i. _____
Stockholders' Equity			
Unrealized gain (loss) on available-for-sale investments	d. _____	f. _____	(11,000)
Retained earnings	$151,000	$201,000	j. _____

EXERCISE 15-20

a.

JOURNAL

	DATE	DESCRIPTION	POST. REF.	DEBIT	CREDIT
1					
2					
3					
4					
5					
6					
7					
8					
9					
10					
11					
12					
13					
14					
15					
16					
17					
18					
19					
20					

b. _____
_____
_____
_____
_____
_____
_____

Name _____ Chapter 15 609

EXERCISE 15-21

a.

JOURNAL   PAGE

DATE		DESCRIPTION	POST. REF.	DEBIT	CREDIT	
						1
						2
						3
						4
						5
						6
						7
						8
						9
						10
						11
						12
						13
						14
						15

b. _____

_____

_____

_____

_____

_____

_____

EXERCISE 15-22

a.

JOURNAL   PAGE

DATE		DESCRIPTION	POST. REF.	DEBIT	CREDIT	
						1
						2
						3
						4
						5
						6
						7

© 2012 Cengage Learning. All Rights Reserved. May not be scanned, copied or duplicated, or posted to a publicly accessible website, in whole or in part.

EXERCISE 15-22, Concluded

Computations:

b.

EXERCISE 15-23

a.

Balance Sheet (selected items)

EXERCISE 15-23, Concluded

b.

Balance Sheet (selected items)

EXERCISE 15-24

Stockholders' Equity

APPENDIX EXERCISE 15-25

Statement of Comprehensive Income

APPENDIX EXERCISE 15-26

Statement of Comprehensive Income

EXERCISE 15-27

Dividend Yield: _____

_____
_____
_____
_____

EXERCISE 15-28

a. **2008: Dividend Yield:** _____

   2009: Dividend Yield: _____

b. _____
_____
_____
_____
_____
_____
_____
_____
_____
_____
_____

EXERCISE 15-29

_____
_____
_____
_____
_____
_____
_____
_____

This Page Not Used.

PROBLEM 15-1 ___

1.

JOURNAL

PAGE

DATE	DESCRIPTION	POST. REF.	DEBIT	CREDIT
2012				

PROBLEM 15-1 ___, Concluded

2.

PROBLEM 15-2 ___

1.

JOURNAL PAGE

	DATE	DESCRIPTION	POST. REF.	DEBIT	CREDIT	
1	2012					1
2						2
3						3
4						4
5						5
6						6
7						7
8						8
9						9
10						10
11						11
12						12
13						13
14						14
15						15
16						16
17						17
18						18
19						19
20						20
21						21
22						22
23						23

Calculations:

PROBLEM 15-2 ___, Continued

1.

JOURNAL   PAGE

	DATE	DESCRIPTION	POST. REF.	DEBIT	CREDIT	
1	2013					1
2						2
3						3
4						4
5						5
6						6
7						7
8						8
9						9
10						10
11						11
12						12
13						13
14						14
15						15
16						16
17						17
18						18
19						19

PROBLEM 15-2 ___, Concluded

2.

Balance Sheet (selected items)

3. _____

This Page Not Used.

PROBLEM 15-3 ___

1.

JOURNAL

PAGE ___

	DATE	DESCRIPTION	POST. REF.	DEBIT	CREDIT	
1	2012					1

PROBLEM 15-3 ___, Continued

JOURNAL PAGE

	DATE	DESCRIPTION	POST. REF.	DEBIT	CREDIT	
1	2013					1
2						2
3						3
4						4
5						5
6						6
7						7
8						8
9						9
10						10
11						11
12						12
13						13
14						14
15						15
16						16
17						17
18						18
19						19
20						20
21						21
22						22
23						23
24						24

PROBLEM 15-3 ___, Concluded

2.

Balance Sheet (selected items)

This Page Not Used.

Name _____

Chapter 15 625

PROBLEM 15-4 ___

1. a. _____
   b. _____
   c. _____

Calculations:

d. _____
e. _____
f. _____
g. _____
h. _____
i. _____

PROBLEM 15-4 ___, Continued

Completed comparative unclassified balance sheet (optional):

Balance Sheet

	DEC. 31, 2013	DEC. 31, 2012

For December 31, 2013:

PROBLEM 15-4 ___, Concluded

For December 31, 2013:

This Page Not Used.

COMPREHENSIVE PROBLEM 4

1.

JOURNAL

PAGE

DATE	DESCRIPTION	POST. REF.	DEBIT	CREDIT

COMPREHENSIVE PROBLEM 4, Continued

JOURNAL

PAGE

	DATE	DESCRIPTION	POST. REF.	DEBIT	CREDIT	
1						1
2						2
3						3
4						4
5						5
6						6
7						7
8						8
9						9
10						10
11						11
12						12
13						13
14						14
15						15
16						16
17						17
18						18
19						19
20						20
21						21
22						22
23						23
24						24
25						25
26						26
27						27
28						28
29						29
30						30
31						31
32						32
33						33
34						34
35						35
36						36

COMPREHENSIVE PROBLEM 4, Continued

JOURNAL

PAGE

	DATE	DESCRIPTION	POST. REF.	DEBIT	CREDIT	
1						1
2						2
3						3
4						4
5						5
6						6
7						7
8						8
9						9
10						10
11						11
12						12
13						13
14						14
15						15
16						16
17						17
18						18
19						19
20						20
21						21
22						22
23						23
24						24
25						25
26						26
27						27
28						28
29						29
30						30
31						31
32						32
33						33
34						34
35						35
36						36

COMPREHENSIVE PROBLEM 4, Continued

2. a.

Income Statement

COMPREHENSIVE PROBLEM 4, Continued

b.

Retained Earnings Statement

COMPREHENSIVE PROBLEM 4, Continued

c.

Balance Sheet

COMPREHENSIVE PROBLEM 4, Concluded

Balance Sheet (continued)

This Page Not Used.

EXERCISE 16-1

_____
_____
_____
_____
_____
_____
_____
_____
_____
_____

EXERCISE 16-2

a. _____
b. _____
c. _____
d. _____
e. _____
f. _____
g. _____
h. _____

EXERCISE 16-3

a. Sold equipment: _____
b. Issued bonds: _____
c. Issued common stock: _____
d. Paid cash dividends: _____
e. Purchased treasury stock: _____
f. Redeemed bonds: _____
g. Purchased patents: _____
h. Purchased buildings: _____
i. Sold long-term investments: _____
j. Issued preferred stock: _____
k. Net income: _____

EXERCISE 16-4

a. Decrease in accounts payable: _____

b. Increase in notes receivable due in 90 days from customers: _____

c. Decrease in accounts receivable: _____

d. Loss on disposal of fixed assets: _____

e. Increase in notes payable due in 90 days to vendors: _____

f. Amortization of patent: _____

g. Depreciation of fixed assets: _____

h. Gain on retirement of long-term debt: _____

i. Decrease in salaries payable: _____

j. Increase in merchandise receivable: _____

k. Decrease in prepaid expenses: _____

EXERCISE 16-5

a.

EXERCISE 16-5, Concluded

b.

Name _____ Chapter 16

EXERCISE 16-6

a.

b. _____

EXERCISE 16-7

a.

EXERCISE 16-7, Concluded

b.

EXERCISE 16-8

EXERCISE 16-9

EXERCISE 16-10

EXERCISE 16-11

EXERCISE 16-12

EXERCISE 16-13

EXERCISE 16-14

EXERCISE 16-15

a.

b.

EXERCISE 16-16

a.

Cash Flows from Operating Activities

b.

EXERCISE 16-17

a.

Statement of Cash Flows

EXERCISE 16-17, Concluded

b.

EXERCISE 16-18

EXERCISE 16-18, Concluded
(Optional)

Statement of Cash Flows

EXERCISE 16-19

a.

b.

c.

EXERCISE 16-20

EXERCISE 16-21

a.

b.

EXERCISE 16-22

a.

Computations:

b.

EXERCISE 16-23

Computations:

EXERCISE 16-24

a.

b.

EXERCISE 16-25

a.

	FISCAL YEAR ENDED MAY 31, 2010 (all numbers in thousands)

EXERCISE 16-25, Concluded

b.

c.

EXERCISE 16-26

This Page Not Used.

PROBLEM 16-1 ___

Statement of Cash Flows

PROBLEM 16-1 ___, Concluded

The use of this form is not required unless so indicated by the instructor.

	A	B	C	D	E
1					
2		Spreadsheet (Work Sheet) for Statement of Cash Flows			
3					
4			Transactions		
5		Balance, _____	Debit	Credit	Balance, _____
6					

PROBLEM 16-2 ___

Statement of Cash Flows

PROBLEM 16-2 ___, Continued

The use of this form is not required unless so indicated by the instructor.

	A	B	C	D	E
1					
2		Spreadsheet (Work Sheet) for Statement of Cash Flows			
3					
4			Transactions		
5		Balance, _____	Debit	Credit	Balance, _____

PROBLEM 16-2 ___, Concluded

The use of this form is not required unless so indicated by the instructor.

	A	B	C	D	E
1					
2		Spreadsheet (Work Sheet) for Statement of Cash Flows			
3					
4			Transactions		
5		Balance, _____	Debit	Credit	Balance, _____
6					
7					
8					
9					
10					
11					
12					
13					
14					
15					
16					
17					
18					
19					
20					
21					
22					
23					
24					
25					

This Page Not Used.

PROBLEM 16-3 ___

Statement of Cash Flows

PROBLEM 16-3 ___, Concluded

The use of this form is not required unless so indicated by the instructor.

	Balance, _____	Transactions		Balance, _____
		Debit	Credit	

PROBLEM 16-4 ___

	Statement of Cash Flows			

PROBLEM 16-4 ___, Concluded

Statement of Cash Flows (continued)

Computations:

PROBLEM 16-5 ___

Statement of Cash Flows

PROBLEM 16-5 ___, Concluded

Statement of Cash Flows (continued)

Computations:

EXERCISE 17-1

a.

Comparative Income Statement

	2012		2011	
	AMOUNT	PERCENT	AMOUNT	PERCENT

b.

EXERCISE 17-2

a.

Comparative Income Statement (in thousands of dollars)

	2008		2007	
	AMOUNT	PERCENT	AMOUNT	PERCENT

b.

EXERCISE 17-3

a.

Common-Sized Income Statement

	SHOESMITH ELECTRONICS COMPANY		ELECTRONICS INDUSTRY AVERAGE
	AMOUNT	PERCENT	

b.

EXERCISE 17-4

Comparative Balance Sheet

	2012		2011	
	AMOUNT	PERCENT	AMOUNT	PERCENT

EXERCISE 17-5

a.

Comparative Income Statement

	2012 AMOUNT	2011 AMOUNT	INCREASE (DECREASE)	
			AMOUNT	PERCENT

b.

Name _____ Chapter 17 673

EXERCISE 17-6

a. (1) Working Capital = _____

2012: _____

2011: _____

(2) Current Ratio = _____

2012: _____

2011: _____

(3) Quick Ratio = _____

2012: _____

2011: _____

b. _____

EXERCISE 17-7

a. (1) Current Ratio = _____

Dec. 26, 2009: _____

Dec. 27, 2008: _____

EXERCISE 17-7, Concluded

(2) Quick Ratio = _____

Dec. 26, 2009: _____

Dec. 27, 2008: _____

b. _____

EXERCISE 17-8

a. _____

The correct calculations are:

Working Capital = _____

Current Ratio = _____

Quick Ratio = _____

Name _____   Chapter 17   675

EXERCISE 17-8, Concluded

b. _____

_____

_____

_____

_____

_____

EXERCISE 17-9

a. (1) Accounts Receivable Turnover = _____

_____

   2012: _____

_____

   2011: _____

_____

   (2) Number of Days' Sales in Receivables = _____

_____

   2012: _____

_____

   2011: _____

_____

_____

_____

_____

_____

b. _____

_____

_____

_____

_____

_____

_____

_____

_____

EXERCISE 17-10

a. (1) Accounts Receivable Turnover = _____

Klick: _____

Klack: _____

(2) Number of Days' Sales in Receivables = _____

Klick: _____

Klack: _____

b. _____

EXERCISE 17-11

a. (1) Inventory Turnover = _____

Current Year: _____

Preceding Year: _____

EXERCISE 17-11, Concluded

(2) Number of Days' Sales in Inventory = _____

Current Year: _____

Preceding Year: _____

b. _____

EXERCISE 17-12

a. (1) Inventory Turnover = _____

Dell: _____

HP: _____

(2) Number of Days' Sales in Inventory = _____

Dell: _____

HP: _____

EXERCISE 17-12, Concluded

b. _____

_____

_____

_____

_____

_____

_____

_____

_____

_____

_____

_____

_____

_____

_____

_____

_____

_____

EXERCISE 17-13

a. Ratio of Liabilities to Stockholders' Equity = _____

_____

Dec. 31, 2012: _____

_____

Dec. 31, 2011: _____

_____

b. Number of Times Bond Interest Charges Are Earned = _____

_____

Dec. 31, 2012: _____

_____

Dec. 31, 2011: _____

_____

_____

_____

EXERCISE 17-13, Concluded

c. _____

EXERCISE 17-14

a. Ratio of Liabilities to Stockholders' Equity = _____

   Hasbro: _____

   Mattel, Inc.: _____

b. Number of Times Interest Charges Are Earned = _____

   Hasbro: _____

   Mattel, Inc.: _____

c. _____

EXERCISE 17-15

a. Ratio of Liabilities to Stockholders' Equity = _____

_____

   H. J. Heinz: _____

_____

   Hershey: _____

_____

b. Ratio of Fixed Assets to Long-Term Liabilities = _____

_____

   H. J. Heinz: _____

_____

   Hershey: _____

_____

c. _____

EXERCISE 17-16

a. Ratio of Net Sales to Total Assets = _____

YRC Worldwide: _____

Union Pacific: _____

C. H. Robinson Worldwide Inc.: _____

b.

EXERCISE 17-17

a. Rate Earned on Total Assets = _____

2012: _____

2011: _____

Rate Earned on Stockholders' Equity = _____

2012: _____

2011: _____

Rate Earned on Common Stockholders' Equity = _____

2012: _____

2011: _____

b. _____

EXERCISE 17-18

a. Rate Earned on Total Assets = _____

   Fiscal Year 2007: _____

   Fiscal Year 2006: _____

b. Rate Earned on Stockholders' Equity = _____

   Fiscal Year 2007: _____

   Fiscal Year 2006: _____

c. _____

d. _____

EXERCISE 17-19

a. Ratio of Fixed Assets to Long-Term Liabilities = _____

b. Ratio of Liabilities to Stockholders' Equity = _____

c. Ratio of Net Sales to Assets = _____

d. Rate Earned on Total Assets = _____

e. Rate Earned on Stockholders' Equity = _____

f. Rate Earned on Common Stockholders' Equity = _____

EXERCISE 17-20

a. Number of Times Bond Interest Charges Are Earned = _____

b. Number of Times Preferred Dividends Are Earned = _____

c. Earnings per Share on Common Stock = _____

d. Price-Earnings Ratio = _____

e. Dividends per Share of Common Stock = _____

f. Dividend Yield = _____

EXERCISE 17-21

a. Earnings per Share =

b. Price-Earnings Ratio =

c. Dividends per Share =

d. Dividend Yield =

EXERCISE 17-22

a. Price-Earnings Ratio = _____

The Home Depot: _____

Google: _____

Coca-Cola: _____

Dividend Yield = _____

The Home Depot: _____

Google: _____

Coca-Cola: _____

b. _____

688 Name _____   *Chapter 17*

APPENDIX EXERCISE 17-23

a. Earnings per share on income before extraordinary items:

Earnings Before Extraordinary Items per Share on Common Stock = _____

_____
_____
_____
_____
_____

b. Earnings per Share on Common Stock = _____

_____
_____
_____
_____

APPENDIX EXERCISE 17-24

a. _____
b. _____
c. _____
d. _____
e. _____
f. _____
g. _____

APPENDIX EXERCISE 17-25

a.

Partial Income Statement

b.

Partial Income Statement

APPENDIX EXERCISE 17-26

a.

b.

PROBLEM 17-1 ___

1.

Comparative Income Statement

	2012	2011	INCREASE (DECREASE)	
			AMOUNT	PERCENT

2.

This Page Not Used.

PROBLEM 17-2

1.

Comparative Income Statement

	2012		2011	
	AMOUNT	PERCENT	AMOUNT	PERCENT

2.

This Page Not Used.

PROBLEM 17-3 ___

1. **a.** Working Capital = _____

   _____

   _____

   _____

   _____

   b. Current Ratio = _____

   _____

   _____

   _____

   _____

   c. Quick Ratio = _____

   _____

   _____

   _____

   _____

PROBLEM 17-3 ___, Concluded

2.

Transaction	Working Capital	Current Ratio	Quick Ratio
a.			
b.			
c.			
d.			
e.			
f.			
g.			
h.			
i.			
j.			

Supporting calculations:

Transaction	Current Assets	Quick Assets	Current Liabilities
a.			
b.			
c.			
d.			
e.			
f.			
g.			
h.			
i.			
j.			

Name _____ Chapter 17 697

PROBLEM 17-4 ___

1. through 19.

1. Working Capital: _____

Ratio	Numerator	Denominator	Calculated Value
2. Current ratio			
3. Quick ratio			
4. Accounts receivable turnover			
5. Number of days' sales in receivables			
6. Inventory turnover			
7. Number of days' sales in inventory			
8. Ratio of fixed assets to long-term liabilities			
9. Ratio of liabilities to stockholders' equity			
10. Number of times interest charges earned			
11. Number of times preferred dividends earned			
12. Ratio of net sales to assets			
13. Rate earned on total assets			
14. Rate earned on stockholders' equity			
15. Rate earned on common stockholders' equity			
16. Earnings per share on common stock			

PROBLEM 17-4 ___, Concluded

Ratio	Numerator	Denominator	Calculated Value
17. Price-earnings ratio			
18. Dividends per share of common stock			
19. Dividend yield			

PROBLEM 17-5 ___

1. a.

[Graph with y-axis labeled "Rate Earned on Total Assets" and x-axis labeled "Year"]

Rate Earned on Total Assets = _____

2012: _____   2009: _____

2011: _____   2008: _____

2010: _____

PROBLEM 17-5 ___, Continued

1. b.

Rate Earned on Stockholders' Equity

Year

Rate Earned on Stockholders' Equity = _____

2012: _____   2009: _____

2011: _____   2008: _____

2010: _____

PROBLEM 17-5 ___, Continued

1. c.

Number of Times Interest Charges Are Earned

Year

Number of Times Interest Charges Earned =

2012:   2009:

2011:   2008:

2010:

PROBLEM 17-5 ___, Continued

1. d.

<chart: blank grid; y-axis "Ratio of Liabilities to Stockholders' Equity"; x-axis "Year">

Ratio of Liabilities to Stockholders' Equity =
_____

2012:	2009:
2011:	2008:
2010:	

PROBLEM 17-5 ___, Concluded

2.

This Page Not Used.

NIKE, INC., PROBLEM

1. a. through m.

	2009	2008

NIKE, INC., PROBLEM, Continued

	2009	2008

NIKE, INC., PROBLEM, Continued

2. a. through m.

NIKE, INC., PROBLEM, Concluded

Name _____   Chapter 18   709

EXERCISE 18-1

a. Depreciation of welding equipment: _____

b. Assembly machinery lubricants: _____

c. Steering wheel: _____

d. Wages of assembly line worker: _____

e. Tires: _____

f. V8 automobile engine: _____

g. Salary of test driver: _____

h. Steel used in body: _____

EXERCISE 18-2

a. Scents and fragrances: _____

b. Wages paid to Packaging Department employees: _____

c. Resins for soap and shampoo products: _____

d. Maintenance supplies Packaging materials: _____

e. Depreciation on production machinery: _____

f. Salary of process engineers: _____

g. Plant manager salary for the Clarksville, Indiana, soap plant: _____

h. Packaging materials: _____

i. Depreciation on the Morristown, Tennessee, toothpaste plant: _____

j. Wages of production line employees: _____

EXERCISE 18-3

a. Sales incentive fees to dealers: _____

b. Factory supplies used in the Danville, Kentucky, tractor tread plant: _____

c. Depreciation on Peoria, Illinois, headquarters building: _____

d. Interest expense on debt: _____

e. Amortization of patents on new assembly process: _____

f. Steel plate: _____

g. Vice president of finance's salary: _____

h. Property taxes on the Aurora, Illinois, manufacturing plant: _____

i. Plant manager's salary at Aurora, Illinois, manufacturing plant: _____

j. Consultant fees for a study of production line employee productivity: _____

EXERCISE 18-4

a. Advertising expenses: _____

b. Salaries of distribution center personnel: _____

c. Factory janitorial supplies: _____

d. Repairs and maintenance costs for sewing machines: _____

e. Travel costs of media relations employees: _____

f. Fabric used during production: _____

g. Depreciation on office equipment: _____

h. Salary of production quality control supervisor: _____

i. Utility costs for office building: _____

j. Depreciation on sewing machines: _____

k. Factory supervisors' salaries: _____

l. Wages of sewing machine operators: _____

m. Property taxes on factory building and equipment: _____

n. Research and development costs: _____

o. Chief financial officer's salary: _____

p. Sales commissions: _____

q. Oil used to lubricate sewing machines: _____

EXERCISE 18-5

a. _____ e. _____

b. _____ f. _____

c. _____ g. _____

d. _____

Name _____   Chapter 18 711

EXERCISE 18-6

a. _____   e. _____
b. _____   f. _____
c. _____   g. _____
d. _____

EXERCISE 18-7

a. Fuel costs: _____
b. Maintenance costs of right of way, bridges, and buildings: _____
c. Wages of switch and classification yard personnel: _____
d. Cost to lease (rent) train locomotives: _____
e. Wages of train engineers: _____
f. Cost to lease (rent) railroad cars: _____
g. Depreciation of terminal facilities: _____
h. Payroll clerk salaries: _____
i. Safety training costs: _____
j. Cost of track and bed (ballast) replacement: _____
k. Salaries of dispatching and communications personnel: _____
l. Costs of accident cleanup: _____

EXERCISE 18-8

1.

2.

Manufacturing Costs

EXERCISE 18-9

a.

Income Statement

b. Inventory balances on January 31, 20--:

Materials:

Work in Process:

Finished Goods:

EXERCISE 18-10

Balance Sheet

EXERCISE 18-11

EXERCISE 18-12

Work in process inventory, November 1	$ 16,000	$ 36,000	(e) _____
Total manufacturing costs incurred during November	112,000	(c) _____	42,000
Total manufacturing costs	(a) _____	$210,000	$49,000
Work in process inventory, November 30	24,000	48,000	(f) _____
Cost of goods manufactured	(b) _____	(d) _____	$43,000

EXERCISE 18-13

EXERCISE 18-14

Finished goods inventory, November 1	$ 44,000	$ 33,000	(e) _____
Cost of goods manufactured	235,000	(c) _____	404,000
Cost of finished goods available for sale	(a) _____	$186,000	$450,000
Finished goods inventory, November 30	52,000	44,000	(f) _____
Cost of goods sold	(b) _____	(d) _____	$428,000

EXERCISE 18-15

a.

Statement of Cost of Goods Manufactured

b.

EXERCISE 18-16

a., b., and c.

EXERCISE 18-17

a. through e.

PROBLEM 18-1 ___

Cost	Product Costs			Period Costs	
	Direct Materials Cost	Direct Labor Cost	Factory Overhead Cost	Selling Expense	Administrative Expense
a.					
b.					
c.					
d.					
e.					
f.					
g.					
h.					
i.					
j.					
k.					
l.					
m.					
n.					
o.					
p.					
q.					
r.					
s.					
t.					
u.					
v.					
w.					
x.					
y.					
z.					

This Page Not Used.

PROBLEM 18-2 ___

Cost	Product Costs			Period Costs	
	Direct Materials Cost	Direct Labor Cost	Factory Overhead Cost	Selling Expense	Administrative Expense
a.					
b.					
c.					
d.					
e.					
f.					
g.					
h.					
i.					
j.					
k.					
l.					
m.					
n.					
o.					
p.					
q.					
r.					
s.					
t.					
u.					
v.					
w.					
x.					

This Page Not Used.

PROBLEM 18-3 ___

1.

2.

Cost	Direct	Indirect
a.		
b.		
c.		
d.		
e.		
f.		
g.		
h.		
i.		
j.		
k.		
l.		
m.		
n.		
o.		
p.		
q.		
r.		
s.		
t.		
u.		

This Page Not Used.

PROBLEM 18-4 ___

1.

_____ Company   _____ Company

a. _____   a. _____
b. _____   b. _____
c. _____   c. _____
d. _____   d. _____
e. _____   e. _____
f. _____   f. _____

2.

_____
Statement of Cost of Goods Manufactured

PROBLEM 18-4 ___ Concluded

3.

Income Statement

Problem 18-5___

1.

Statement of Cost of Goods Manufactured

PROBLEM 18-5 ___, Concluded

2.

Income Statement

EXERCISE 19-1

a. _____

b. _____

c. _____

d. _____

e. _____

EXERCISE 19-2

a. Cost of goods sold:

b. Direct materials cost:

c. Direct labor cost:

Chapter 19

EXERCISE 19-3

a.

RECEIVED			ISSUED			BALANCE			
Receiving Report Number	Quantity	Unit Price	Materials Requisition Number	Quantity	Amount	Date	Quantity	Unit Price	Amount
						June 1	350	$10.00	$3,500
26	250	$12.00				June 2	_____	_____	_____
							_____	_____	_____
			103	380	_____	June 6	_____	_____	_____
32	160	14.00				June 12	_____	_____	_____
							_____	_____	_____
			111	240	_____	June 21	_____	_____	_____

b. _____

c.

JOURNAL   PAGE

	DATE	DESCRIPTION	POST. REF.	DEBIT	CREDIT	
1						1
2						2
3						3

d. _____

EXERCISE 19-4

JOURNAL   PAGE

	DATE	DESCRIPTION	POST. REF.	DEBIT	CREDIT	
1						1
2						2
3						3
4						4

EXERCISE 19-5

a. and b.

JOURNAL   PAGE

	DATE	DESCRIPTION	POST. REF.	DEBIT	CREDIT	
1						1
2						2
3						3
4						4
5						5
6						6
7						7
8						8

c.

	Fabric	Polyester Filling	Lumber	Glue

Name _____ Chapter 19

EXERCISE 19-6

JOURNAL PAGE

	DATE	DESCRIPTION	POST. REF.	DEBIT	CREDIT	
1						1
2						2
3						3
4						4

EXERCISE 19-7

a.

JOURNAL PAGE

	DATE	DESCRIPTION	POST. REF.	DEBIT	CREDIT	
1						1
2						2
3						3
4						4

Supporting Calculations:

b.

Chapter 19

EXERCISE 19-8

a. and b.

JOURNAL PAGE

	DATE	DESCRIPTION	POST. REF.	DEBIT	CREDIT	
1						1
2						2
3						3
4						4
5						5
6						6
7						7
8						8

EXERCISE 19-9

a. Factory 1 overhead rate: _____

b. Factory 2 overhead rate: _____

c.

JOURNAL PAGE

	DATE	DESCRIPTION	POST. REF.	DEBIT	CREDIT	
1						1
2						2
3						3
4						4
5						5
6						6
7						7
8						8
9						9

d. Balance of Factory 1 accounts as of November 30: _____

Balance of Factory 2 accounts as of November 30: _____

EXERCISE 19-10

EXERCISE 19-11

a.

b.

c.

EXERCISE 19-12

a.

JOURNAL

PAGE

	DATE	DESCRIPTION	POST. REF.	DEBIT	CREDIT	
1						1
2						2
3						3
4						4

b.

Name _____   Chapter 19   737

EXERCISE 19-13

a. through d.

JOURNAL   PAGE _____

	DATE	DESCRIPTION	POST. REF.	DEBIT	CREDIT	
1						1
2						2
3						3
4						4
5						5
6						6
7						7
8						8
9						9
10						10
11						11
12						12
13						13
14						14
15						15
16						16
17						17
18						18
19						19

EXERCISE 19-14

a.

Income Statement

EXERCISE 19-14, Concluded

b.

Materials inventory:

Work in process inventory:

Finished goods inventory:

EXERCISE 19-15

a.

Date	Job No.	Quantity	Product	Amount	Unit Cost
Jan. 2	1	300	XKR1	$ 6,600	_____
Jan. 15	26	1,300	M-Z4	11,700	_____
Feb. 3	34	1,100	M-Z4	14,300	_____
Mar. 7	44	460	XKR1	7,360	_____
Mar. 24	51	1,850	SL500	12,950	_____
May 19	62	2,200	SL500	19,800	_____
June 12	76	400	XKR1	4,800	_____
Aug. 18	80	2,750	SL500	30,250	_____
Sept. 2	88	900	M-Z4	9,000	_____
Nov. 14	96	540	XKR1	4,320	_____
Dec. 12	102	2,350	SL500	32,900	_____

XKR1 Unit Costs

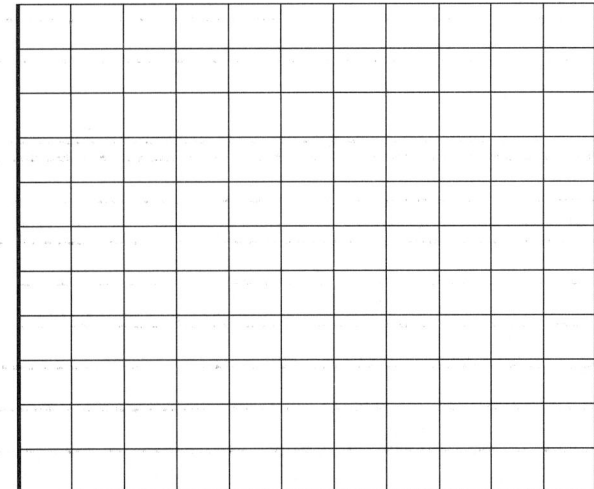

Job Number

EXERCISE 19-15, Continued

M-Z4 Unit Costs

Unit Cost / Job Number

SL500 Unit Costs

Unit Cost / Job Number

_____
_____
_____
_____

EXERCISE 19-15, Concluded

b.

EXERCISE 19-16

a.

EXERCISE 19-16, Concluded

b.

EXERCISE 19-17

a.

JOURNAL   PAGE

	DATE	DESCRIPTION	POST. REF.	DEBIT	CREDIT	

b.

EXERCISE 19-17, Concluded

c.

EXERCISE 19-18

a. through d.

JOURNAL

	DATE	DESCRIPTION	POST. REF.	DEBIT	CREDIT	
1						1
2						2
3						3
4						4
5						5
6						6
7						7
8						8
9						9
10						10
11						11
12						12

Supporting calculations:

PROBLEM 19-1 ___

a. through i.

JOURNAL

PAGE ___

	DATE	DESCRIPTION	POST. REF.	DEBIT	CREDIT	
1						1
2						2
3						3
4						4
5						5
6						6
7						7
8						8
9						9
10						10
11						11
12						12
13						13
14						14
15						15
16						16
17						17
18						18
19						19
20						20
21						21
22						22
23						23
24						24
25						25
26						26
27						27
28						28
29						29
30						30
31						31
32						32
33						33
34						34
35						35
36						36

This Page Not Used.

PROBLEM 19-2 ___

1. a. through g.

JOURNAL

PAGE _____

	DATE	DESCRIPTION	POST. REF.	DEBIT	CREDIT	
1						1
2						2
3						3
4						4
5						5
6						6
7						7
8						8
9						9
10						10
11						11
12						12
13						13
14						14
15						15
16						16
17						17
18						18
19						19
20						20
21						21
22						22
23						23
24						24
25						25
26						26

f. Computation of cost of jobs finished:

PROBLEM 19-2 ___, Concluded

g. Computation of cost of jobs sold:

2.

Work in Process	

Finished Goods	

3.

Schedule of Unfinished Jobs

JOB	DIRECT MATERIALS	DIRECT LABOR	FACTORY OVERHEAD	TOTAL

4.

Schedule of Completed Jobs

JOB	DIRECT MATERIALS	DIRECT LABOR	FACTORY OVERHEAD	TOTAL

PROBLEM 19-3 ___

1. and 2.

JOB ORDER COST SHEET

Customer _____ Date _____

Address _____ Date wanted _____

_____ Date completed _____

Item _____ Job No. _____

ESTIMATE

Direct Materials	Amount	Direct Labor	Amount	Summary	Amount
___ meters at $ ____	_____	___ hours at $ ____	_____	Direct materials	_____
___ meters at ____	_____	___ hours at ____	_____	Direct labor	_____
___ meters at ____	_____	___ hours at ____	_____	Factory overhead	_____
___ meters at ____	_____	___ hours at ____	_____		
Total	_____	Total	_____	Total cost	_____

ACTUAL

Direct Materials			Direct Labor			Summary	
Mat. Req. No.	Description	Amount	Time Ticket No.	Description	Amount	Item	Amount
____	____	____	____	____	____	Direct materials	____
____	____	____	____	____	____	Direct labor	____
____	____	____	____	____	____	Factory overhead	____
Total		____	Total		____	Total cost	____

Comments:

This Page Not Used.

Name _____   Chapter 19

PROBLEM 19-4 ___

1. Supporting calculations:

Job No.	Quan-tity	Work in Process Direct Materials	Direct Labor	Factory Overhead	Total Cost	Unit Cost	Units Sold	Cost of Goods Sold

(A) _____

(B) _____

(C) _____

(D) _____

(E) _____

(F) _____

(G) _____

(H) _____

PROBLEM 19-4 ___, Concluded

2.

Name _____ Chapter 19 753

PROBLEM 19-5 ___

1.

Income Statement

Supporting calculations:

PROBLEM 19-5 ___, Concluded

2.

Name _____   Chapter 20   755

EXERCISE 20-1

a. through e.

JOURNAL   PAGE

	DATE	DESCRIPTION	POST. REF.	DEBIT	CREDIT	
1						1
2						2
3						3
4						4
5						5
6						6
7						7
8						8
9						9
10						10
11						11
12						12
13						13
14						14
15						15
16						16
17						17
18						18
19						19
20						20
21						21
22						22
23						23
24						24
25						25
26						26
27						27
28						28
29						29
30						30
31						31
32						32
33						33
34						34
35						35

© 2012 Cengage Learning. All Rights Reserved. May not be scanned, copied or duplicated, or posted to a publicly accessible website, in whole or in part.

Name _____

Chapter 20

EXERCISE 20-2

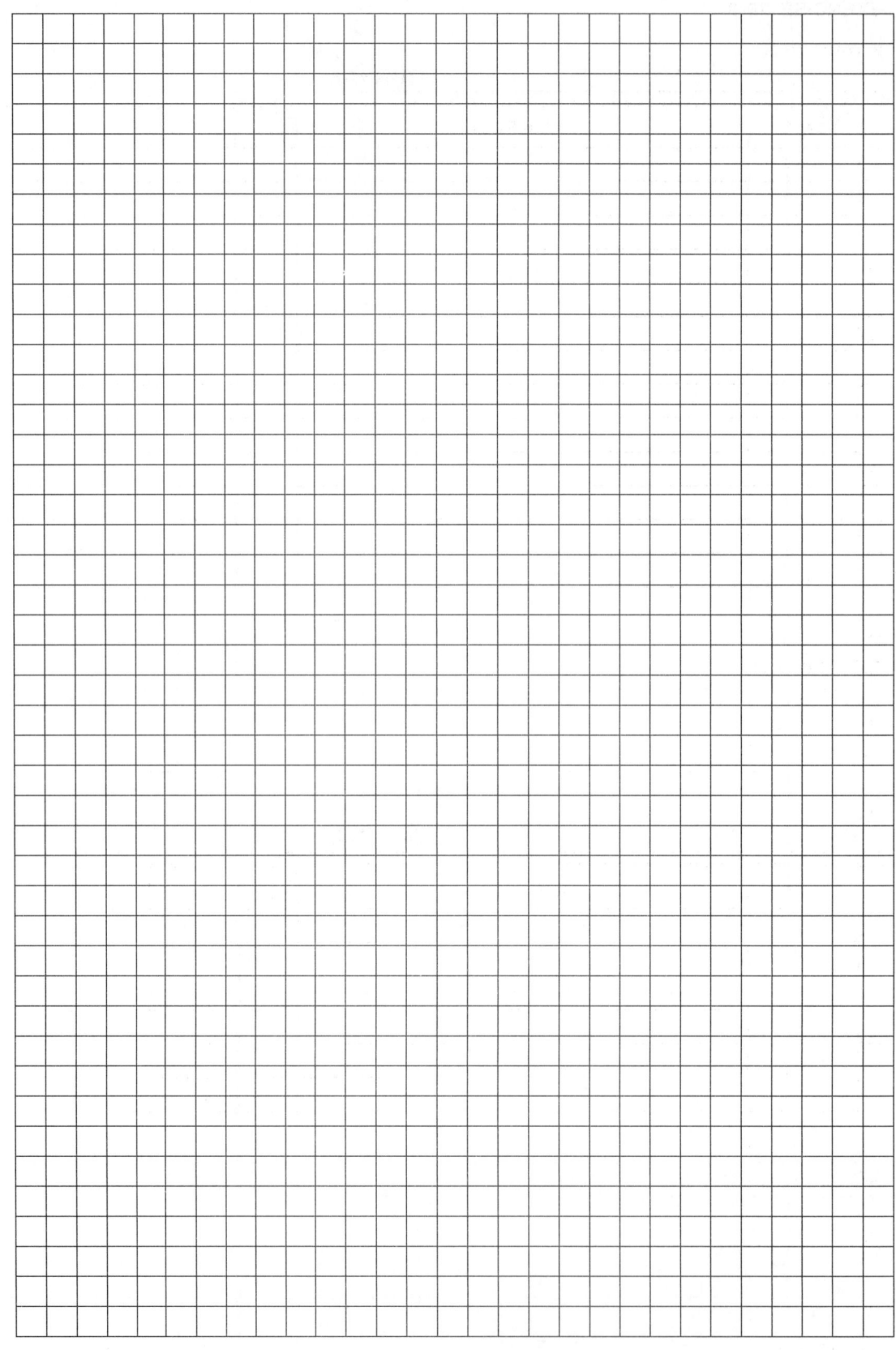

EXERCISE 20-3

a. and b.

JOURNAL PAGE

	DATE	DESCRIPTION	POST. REF.	DEBIT	CREDIT	
1						1
2						2
3						3
4						4
5						5
6						6
7						7
8						8
9						9
10						10
11						11
12						12
13						13

EXERCISE 20-4

a. _____

b.

JOURNAL PAGE

	DATE	DESCRIPTION	POST. REF.	DEBIT	CREDIT	
1						1
2						2
3						3
4						4
5						5
6						6

c. _____

d. _____

Name _____

EXERCISE 20-5

	Whole Units	Equivalent Units	
		Direct Materials	Conversion

EXERCISE 20-6

a. Drawing Department

	Whole Units	Equivalent Units	
		Direct Materials	Conversion

b. Winding Department

	Whole Units	Equivalent Units	
		Direct Materials	Conversion

EXERCISE 20-7

a.

b.

	Whole Units	Equivalent Units	
		Direct Materials	Conversion

EXERCISE 20-8

a.

1. _____
2. _____
3. _____

4. _____

5. _____

b.

_____

EXERCISE 20-9

Equivalent units of production:

	CEREAL (IN POUNDS)	BOXES (IN BOXES)	CONVERSION COST (IN BOXES)

Supporting explanation:

EXERCISE 20-10

a.

b.

c.

EXERCISE 20-11

a.

b.

	Whole Units	Equivalent Units	
		Direct Materials	Conversion

c.

	Costs	
	Direct Materials	Conversion

d. _____

EXERCISE 20-12

a.

1. _____

2.

3. _____

4. _____

b.

EXERCISE 20-12, Concluded

c.

EXERCISE 20-13

EXERCISE 20-14

a. _____

b.

A	B	C	D
		Equivalent Units	
	Whole Units	Direct Materials	Conversion

A	B	C
	Costs	
	Direct Materials	Conversion

c. _____

EXERCISE 20-15

a. _____

b. _____

c. _____

d. _____

e. _____

EXERCISE 20-16

a. through d.

	A	B	C	D
1				
2	Cost of Production Report—			
3				
4			Equivalent Units	
5	Units	Whole Units	Direct Materials	Conversion

EXERCISE 20-16, Concluded

	Costs		
Costs	Direct Materials	Conversion	Total

e.

EXERCISE 20-17

a.

Units	Whole Units	Equivalent Units	
		Direct Materials	Conversion

Cost of Production Report—_____

EXERCISE 20-17, Concluded

	Costs		
Costs	Direct Materials	Conversion	Total

b. _____

772 Name _____ Chapter 20

EXERCISE 20-18

a. 1. through 3.

JOURNAL PAGE

	DATE	DESCRIPTION	POST. REF.	DEBIT	CREDIT	
1						1
2						2
3						3
4						4
5						5
6						6
7						7
8						8
9						9
10						10

Supporting calculations:

	A	B	C	D
1			Equivalent Units	
2		Whole Units	Materials	Conversion
3				
4				
5				
6				
7				
8				
9				

b.

EXERCISE 20-18, Concluded

c.

EXERCISE 20-19

a. 1. through 3.

JOURNAL

	DATE	DESCRIPTION	POST. REF.	DEBIT	CREDIT
1					
2					
3					
4					
5					
6					
7					
8					
9					
10					

Supporting calculations:

	A	B	C	D
1			Equivalent Units	
2		Whole Units	Materials	Conversion
3				
4				
5				
6				
7				
8				
9				

b.

EXERCISE 20-20

EXERCISE 20-20, Concluded

EXERCISE 20-21

a.

	A	B	C	D	E	F	G
1		January	February	March	April	May	June
2							
3							
4							
5							

b.

EXERCISE 20-22

APPENDIX EXERCISE 20-23

a. and b.

	A	B a. Whole Units	C b. Equivalent Units of Production
1			
2			
3			
4			
5			
6			
7			
8			
9			
10			
11			
12			
13			
14			
15			
16			

APPENDIX EXERCISE 20-24

a. Drawing Department

	A	B Whole Units	C Equivalent Units of Production
1			
2			
3			
4			
5			
6			
7			
8			
9			
10			
11			
12			
13			
14			
15			
16			

APPENDIX EXERCISE 20-24, Concluded

b. Winding Department

	Whole Units	Equivalent Units of Production

APPENDIX EXERCISE 20-25

a.

b.

	Whole Units	Equivalent Units of Production

APPENDIX EXERCISE 20-26

a. and b.

	Whole Units	Equivalent Units of Production

c.

d.

e.

APPENDIX EXERCISE 20-27

a.

	Whole Units	Equivalent Units of Production

b. _____

c. _____

APPENDIX EXERCISE 20-28

Cost of Production Report—Roasting Department

Units	Whole Units	Equivalent Units of Production

Costs	

APPENDIX EXERCISE 20-29

	A	B	C
1			
2	Cost of Production Report—Cutting Department		
3			
4	Units	Whole Units	Equivalent Units of Production
5			
6			
7			
8			
9			
10			
11			
12			
13			
14			
15			
16			

	A	B
1	Costs	
2		
3		
4		
5		
6		
7		
8		
9		
10		
11		
12		
13		
14		
15		
16		

This Page Not Used.

PROBLEM 20-1 ___

1. a. through i.

JOURNAL

	DATE	DESCRIPTION	POST. REF.	DEBIT	CREDIT	
1						1
2						2
3						3
4						4
5						5
6						6
7						7
8						8
9						9
10						10
11						11
12						12
13						13
14						14
15						15
16						16
17						17
18						18
19						19
20						20
21						21
22						22
23						23
24						24
25						25
26						26
27						27
28						28
29						29
30						30
31						31
32						32
33						33
34						34
35						35
36						36

PROBLEM 20-1 ___, Concluded

JOURNAL   PAGE

	DATE	DESCRIPTION	POST. REF.	DEBIT	CREDIT	
1						1
2						2
3						3
4						4
5						5
6						6

2.

	MATERIALS	WORK IN PROCESS— _____DEPT.	WORK IN PROCESS— _____DEPT.	FINISHED GOODS

3.

	FACTORY OVERHEAD— _____DEPT.	FACTORY OVERHEAD— _____DEPT.

PROBLEM 20-2 ___

1.

		Equivalent Units	
Units	Whole Units	Direct Materials	Conversion

Cost of Production Report—_____

PROBLEM 20-2___, Continued

	A	B	C	D
1		Costs		
2	Costs	Direct Materials	Conversion	Total
3				
4				
5				
6				
7				
8				
9				
10				
11				
12				
13				
14				
15				
16				
17				
18				
19				
20				
21				
22				
23				
24				
25				
26				
27				
28				
29				
30				
31				
32				
33				
34				
35				
36				
37				
38				
39				

PROBLEM 20-2___, Concluded

2.

This Page Not Used.

PROBLEM 20-3 ___

1.

	A	B	C	D
1				
2	Cost of Production Report—_____			
3				
4			Equivalent Units	
5	Units	Whole Units	Direct Materials	Conversion
6				

PROBLEM 20-3___, Continued

	Costs		
Costs	Direct Materials	Conversion	Total

PROBLEM 20-3 ___, Concluded

2.

JOURNAL

PAGE

	DATE	DESCRIPTION	POST. REF.	DEBIT	CREDIT	
1						1
2						2
3						3
4						4
5						5
6						6
7						7
8						8
9						9
10						10

3.

4.

This Page Not Used.

PROBLEM 20-4 ___

1. and 2.

ACCOUNT	Work in Process—_____ Department			ACCOUNT NO.	
DATE	ITEM	DEBIT	CREDIT	BALANCE DEBIT	BALANCE CREDIT

PROBLEM 20-4 ___, Continued

1.

			Equivalent Units	
Units	Whole Units	Direct Materials (a)	Conversion (a)

Cost of Production Report—_____

PROBLEM 20-4___, Continued

	Costs		
Costs	Direct Materials	Conversion	Total

PROBLEM 20-4 ___, Continued

2.

	A	B	C	D
1				
2	Cost of Production Report—_____			
3				
4			Equivalent Units	
5	Units	Whole Units	Direct Materials (a)	Conversion (a)
6				
7				
8				
9				
10				
11				
12				
13				
14				
15				
16				
17				
18				
19				
20				
21				
22				
23				
24				
25				
26				
27				
28				
29				
30				
31				
32				
33				
34				
35				
36				
37				
38				
39				
40				
41				
42				

PROBLEM 20-4___, Continued

	Costs		
Costs	Direct Materials	Conversion	Total

PROBLEM 20-4 ___, Concluded

3.

APPENDIX PROBLEM 20-5___

	A	B	C
1			
2	Cost of Production Report—_____		
3			
4	Units	Whole Units	Equivalent Units of Production
5			
6			
7			
8			
9			
10			
11			
12			
13			
14			
15			
16			
17			
18			
19			

	A	B
1	Costs	
2		
3		
4		
5		
6		
7		
8		
9		
10		
11		
12		
13		
14		
15		
16		

This Page Not Used.

Name _____ Chapter 21

EXERCISE 21-1

1. _____   9. _____
2. _____   10. _____
3. _____   11. _____
4. _____   12. _____
5. _____   13. _____
6. _____   14. _____
7. _____   15. _____
8. _____

EXERCISE 21-2

a. _____   d. _____
b. _____   e. _____
c. _____

EXERCISE 21-3

1. Financial aid office salaries: _____
2. School supplies: _____
3. Instructor salaries: _____
4. Housing personnel wages: _____
5. Student records office salaries: _____
6. Admissions office salaries: _____

EXERCISE 21-4

1. Preparation costs: _____
2. Salespersons' commission: _____
3. Administrative costs: _____

EXERCISE 21-5

a. _____   g. _____
b. _____   h. _____
c. _____   i. _____
d. _____   j. _____
e. _____   k. _____
f. _____   l. _____

EXERCISE 21-6

Components produced	300,000		360,000		375,000
Total costs:					
Total variable costs	$ 75,000	(d) _____		(j) _____	
Total fixed costs	90,000	(e) _____		(k) _____	
Total costs	$165,000	(f) _____		(l) _____	
Cost per unit:					
Variable cost per unit	(a) _____	(g) _____		(m) _____	
Fixed cost per unit	(b) _____	(h) _____		(n) _____	
Total cost per unit	(c) _____	(i) _____		(o) _____	

Supporting calculations:

EXERCISE 21-7

a. Variable cost per unit: _____

Fixed cost: _____

b. _____

EXERCISE 21-8

Variable Cost per Gross-Ton Mile:

Fixed Cost:

EXERCISE 21-9

a.

EXERCISE 21-9, Concluded

b.

EXERCISE 21-10

a.

b.

c.

Name _____

EXERCISE 21-11

a.

b.

EXERCISE 21-12

a.

b.

EXERCISE 21-13

a.

b.

EXERCISE 21-14

EXERCISE 21-15

EXERCISE 21-16

a.

b.

EXERCISE 21-17

a.

Sales and Cost

Units of Sales

b. _____
_____
_____
_____

c. _____
_____
_____
_____
_____
_____
_____

EXERCISE 21-18

a. _____

b.

c.

Operating Profit (Loss)

Units of Sales

d. _____

EXERCISE 21-19

Chart name: _____

a. _____
b. _____
c. _____
d. _____
e. _____
f. _____

EXERCISE 21-20

Chart name: _____

a. _____
b. _____
c. _____
d. _____
e. _____
f. _____

EXERCISE 21-21

a. _____
_____
_____
_____
_____
_____
_____
_____
_____
_____
_____
_____
_____

b. Baseball bats: _____
_____

Baseball gloves: _____
_____

EXERCISE 21-22

a.

b.

Name _____

EXERCISE 21-23

a. (1) In dollars: _____

(2) As a percentage of sales: _____

b. _____

EXERCISE 21-24

EXERCISE 21-25

a. Fulp Inc. operating leverage:

Baucom Inc. operating leverage:

b.

c.

APPENDIX EXERCISE 21-26

a.
b.
c.

APPENDIX EXERCISE 21-27

Income Statement—Variable Costing

Computations:

APPENDIX EXERCISE 21-28

	Income Statement—Absorption Costing		

Computations:

This Page Not Used.

Name _____ Chapter 21 821

PROBLEM 21-1 ___

Cost	Fixed Cost	Variable Cost	Mixed Cost
a.			
b.			
c.			
d.			
e.			
f.			
g.			
h.			
i.			
j.			
k.			
l.			
m.			
n.			
o.			
p.			
q.			
r.			
s.			
t.			

This Page Not Used.

PROBLEM 21-2 ___

1.

	FIXED COSTS	VARIABLE COSTS

2. a. Unit variable cost: _____

b. Unit contribution margin: _____

3.

4.

5.

PROBLEM 21-2 ___, Concluded

6.

7.

8.

PROBLEM 21-3 ___

1. Break-even sales (units):

2. Sales (units):

PROBLEM 21-3 ___, Concluded

3.

Sales and Costs

Units of Sales

4. _____
_____
_____
_____

PROBLEM 21-4 ___

1.

Sales and Costs

Units of Sales

PROBLEM 21-4 ___, Continued

2.

Sales and Costs

Units of Sales

Name _____   Chapter 21 829

PROBLEM 21-4 ___, Continued

3.

Sales and Costs

Units of Sales

PROBLEM 21-4 ___, Concluded

4.

Sales and Costs

Units of Sales

PROBLEM 21-5 ___

1.

2.

3.

This Page Not Used.

PROBLEM 21-6

1.

Estimated Income Statement

PROBLEM 21-6 ___, Continued

2.

3.

PROBLEM 21-6 ___, Continued

4.

Sales and Costs

Units Costs

PROBLEM 21-6 ___, Concluded

5.

6.

EXERCISE 22-1

a.

	A	B	C	D	E
1		CANDACE THOMPSON			
2		Cash Budget			
3		For the Four Months Ending December 31, 2012			
4		September	October	November	December
5					
6					
7					
8					
9					
10					
11					
12					
13					
14					
15					
16					
17					
18					
19					

b.

c.

EXERCISE 22-2

	A	B	C	D
1	NET VISION			
2	Flexible Selling and Administrative Expenses Budget			
3	For the Month Ending January 31, 2012			
4				
5				
6				
7				
8				
9				
10				
11				
12				
13				
14				
15				
16				
17				
18				
19				
20				
21				
22				
23				

EXERCISE 22-3

a.

	A	B	C	D
1	CRAMER COMPANY—MACHINING DEPARTMENT			
2	Flexible Production Budget			
3	For the Three Months Ending March 31, 20XX			
4		January	February	March
5				
6				
7				
8				
9				
10				
11				
12				
13				
14				
15				
16				
17				
18				
19				
20				
21				
22				

b.

	JANUARY	FEBRUARY	MARCH

EXERCISE 22-4

	A	B	C	D
1	STEELCASE INC.—FABRICATION DEPARTMENT			
2	Flexible Production Budget			
3	October 2012			
4	(assumed data)			
5				
6				
7				
8				
9				
10				
11				
12				
13				
14				
15				
16				
17				
18				
19				
20				
21				
22				
23				
24				

EXERCISE 22-5

	A	B	C
1	RITE WEIGHT, INC.		
2	Production Budget		
3	For the Month Ending May 31, 2013		
4		Units	
5		Small Scale	Large Scale
6			
7			
8			
9			
10			
11			
12			
13			

EXERCISE 22-6

a.

	A	B	C	D
1	AUDIO MECHANICS, INC.			
2	Sales Budget			
3	For the Month Ending September 30, 2012			
4	Product and Area	Unit Sales Volume	Unit Selling Price	Total Sales
5				
6				
7				
8				
9				
10				
11				
12				
13				
14				

b.

	A	B	C
1	AUDIO MECHANICS, INC. -		
2	Production Budget		
3	For the Month Ending September 30, 2012		
4		Units	
5		Model DL	Model XL
6			
7			
8			
9			
10			
11			
12			
13			

EXERCISE 22-7

	A	B	C	D
1	PEREZ AND FORD, CPAs			
2	Professional Fees Earned Budget			
3	For the Year Ending December 31, 2012			
4		Billable Hours	Hourly Rate	Total Revenue
5				
6				
7				
8				
9				
10				
11				
12				
13				
14				
15				
16				
17				
18				
19				

EXERCISE 22-8

	A	B	C
1	PEREZ AND FORD, CPAs		
2	Professional Labor Cost Budget		
3	For the Year Ending December 31, 2012		
4		Staff	Partners
5			
6			
7			
8			
9			
10			
11			
12			

EXERCISE 22-9

	A	B	C	D	E
1	ROMANO'S FROZEN PIZZA INC.				
2	Direct Materials Purchases Budget				
3	For the Month Ending June 30, 2012				
4		Dough	Tomato	Cheese	Total
5					
6					
7					
8					
9					
10					
11					
12					
13					
14					
15					
16					
17					
18					
19					
20					
21					
22					

EXERCISE 22-10

	Concentrate	2-Liter Bottles	Carbonated Water
COCA-COLA ENTERPRISES—WAKEFIELD PLANT			
Direct Materials Purchases Budget			
For the Month Ending March 31, 2012			
(assumed data)			

EXERCISE 22-11

	A	B	C	D
1	SAFE RIDE TIRE COMPANY			
2	Direct Materials Purchases Budget			
3	For the Year Ending December 31, 2012			
4		Rubber	Steel Belts	Total
5				
6				
7				
8				
9				
10				
11				
12				
13				
14				
15				
16				
17				
18				
19				

EXERCISE 22-12

	A	B	C
1	ACE RACKET COMPANY		
2	Direct Labor Cost Budget		
3	For the Month Ending May 31, 2012		
4		Forming Department	Assembly Department
5			
6			
7			
8			
9			
10			
11			
12			
13			
14			
15			
16			

EXERCISE 22-13

	EXECUTIVE INN, INC.		
	Direct Labor Cost Budget		
	For a Weekday or a Weekend Day		
		Weekday	Weekend Day

EXERCISE 22-14

a.

	A	B	C
1	LEVI STRAUSS & CO.		
2	Production Budget		
3	March 2012		
4	(assumed data)		
5		Dockers®	501 Jeans®
6			
7			
8			
9			
10			
11			
12			
13			

b.

	A	B	C	D	E	F
1	LEVI STRAUSS & CO.					
2	Direct Labor Cost Budget					
3	March 2012					
4	(assumed data)					
5		Inseam	Outerseam	Pockets	Zipper	Total
6						
7						
8						
9						
10						
11						
12						
13						
14						
15						
16						
17						
18						
19						
20						
21						

EXERCISE 22-15

A	B	C
BLONDIE CANDY COMPANY		
Factory Overhead Cost Budget		
For the Month Ending July 31, 2012		

EXERCISE 22-16

	A	B	C	D
1	DOVER CHEMICAL COMPANY			
2	Cost of Goods Sold Budget			
3	For the Month Ending April 30, 2013			
4				
5				
6				
7				
8				
9				
10				
11				
12				
13				
14				
15				
16				
17				
18				
19				
20				
21				
22				
23				
24				
25				
26				
27				
28				

EXERCISE 22-17

	A	B	C	D
1	ORIENTAL CERAMICS INC.			
2	Cost of Goods Sold Budget			
3	For the Month Ending June 30, 2012			
4				
5				
6				
7				
8				
9				
10				
11				
12				
13				
14				
15				
16				
17				
18				
19				
20				
21				
22				
23				

EXERCISE 22-18

	A	B	C	D
1	PET MART WHOLESALE INC.			
2	Schedule of Collections from Sales			
3	For the Three Months Ending May 31, 2012			
4		March	April	May
5				
6				
7				
8				
9				
10				
11				
12				
13				
14				
15				
16				
17				
18				
19				
20				
21				
22				
23				
24				

EXERCISE 22-19

	A	B	C	D
1		OFFICE UNIVERSE SUPPLIES INC.		
2		Schedule of Collections from Sales		
3		For the Three Months Ending October 31, 2012		
4		August	September	October
5				
6				
7				
8				
9				
10				
11				
12				
13				
14				
15				
16				
17				
18				
19				
20				
21				
22				
23				
24				

EXERCISE 22-20

	A	B	C	D
1		SAGE LEARNING SYSTEMS INC.		
2		Schedule of Cash Payments for Selling and Administrative Expenses		
3		For the Three Months Ending December 31, 2012		
4		October	November	December
5				
6				
7				
8				
9				
10				
11				
12				
13				
14				
15				
16				
17				
18				
19				

EXERCISE 22-21

	A	B	C	D
1		SELECT PHYSICAL THERAPY INC.		
2		Schedule of Cash Payments for Operations		
3		For the Three Months Ending September 30, 2013		
4		July	August	September
5				
6				
7				
8				
9				
10				
11				
12				
13				
14				
15				
16				

EXERCISE 22-22

	2012	2013	2014	2015
MED-TEK INC.				
Capital Expenditures Budget				
For the Four Years Ending December 31, 2012–2015				

PROBLEM 22-1 ___

1.

	UNIT SALES, YEAR ENDED 2012		INCREASE (DECREASE) ACTUAL OVER BUDGET	
	BUDGET	ACTUAL SALES	AMOUNT	PERCENT

2.

	2012 ACTUAL UNITS	PERCENTAGE INCREASE (DECREASE)	2013 BUDGETED UNITS (ROUNDED)

PROBLEM 22-1 ___, Concluded

3.

	Product and Area	Unit Sales Volume	Unit Selling Price	Total Sales
1				
2	Sales Budget			
3				
4				
5				
6				
7				
8				
9				
10				
11				
12				
13				
14				
15				
16				
17				
18				
19				

PROBLEM 22-2 ___

1.

	A	B	C	D
1				
2	Sales Budget			
3				
4	Product and Area	Unit Sales Volume	Unit Selling Price	Total Sales
5				
6				
7				
8				
9				
10				
11				
12				
13				
14				
15				
16				
17				
18				
19				

2.

	A	B	C
1			
2	Production Budget		
3			
4		Units	
5			
6			
7			
8			
9			
10			
11			
12			
13			
14			
15			

PROBLEM 22-2 ___, Continued

3.

	A	B	C	D	E	F
1						
2		Direct Materials Purchases Budget				
3						
4						
5						
6						
7						
8						
9						
10						
11						
12						
13						
14						
15						
16						
17						
18						
19						
20						
21						
22						
23						
24						

PROBLEM 22-2 ___, Concluded

4.

	A	B	C	D	E
1					
2		Direct Labor Cost Budget			
3					
4		Department	Department	Department	Total
5					
6					
7					
8					
9					
10					
11					
12					
13					
14					
15					
16					
17					
18					
19					

This Page Not Used.

Name _____   Chapter 22 861

PROBLEM 22-3 ___

1.

	A	B	C	D
1				
2		Sales Budget		
3				
4		Unit Sales Volume	Unit Selling Price	Total Sales
5				
6				
7				
8				
9				
10				
11				
12				
13				
14				

2.

	A	B	C
1			
2		Production Budget	
3			
4		Units	
5			
6			
7			
8			
9			
10			
11			
12			
13			
14			
15			

PROBLEM 22-3 ___, Continued

3.

	A	B	C	D
1				
2	**Direct Materials Purchases Budget**			
3				
4				Total
5				
6				
7				
8				
9				
10				
11				
12				
13				
14				
15				
16				
17				
18				
19				

4.

	A	B	C	D
1				
2	**Direct Labor Cost Budget**			
3				
4		Department	Department	Total
5				
6				
7				
8				
9				
10				
11				
12				
13				
14				
15				
16				

PROBLEM 22-3 ___, Continued

5.

	A	B	C
1			
2	Factory Overhead Cost Budget		
3			
4			
5			
6			
7			
8			
9			
10			
11			
12			
13			
14			
15			
16			
17			
18			

PROBLEM 22-3 ___, Continued

6.

	A	B	C	D
1				
2	Cost of Goods Sold Budget			
3				

PROBLEM 22-3 ___, Continued

7.

	Selling and Administrative Expenses Budget		

PROBLEM 22-3 ___, Concluded

8.

A	B	C
Budgeted Income Statement		

PROBLEM 22-4 ___

1.

	A	B	C	D
1				
2	Cash Budget			
3				

PROBLEM 22-4 ___, Concluded

2.

PROBLEM 22-5 ___

1.

A	B	C	D
Budgeted Income Statement			

PROBLEM 22-5 ___, Concluded

2.

	A	B	C	D
1				
2	Budgeted Balance Sheet			
3				
4				

EXERCISE 23-1

Ingredient	Quantity	x	Price	Total
		x		
		x		
		x		

EXERCISE 23-2

a.

b.

EXERCISE 23-3

a.

	A	B
1	PET BOTTLE COMPANY	
2	Manufacturing Cost Budget	
3	For the Month Ended March 31, 2012	
4		Standard Cost at Planned Volume (450,000 Bottles)
5		
6		
7		
8		
9		
10		
11		
12		
13		
14		

b.

	A	B	C	D
1	PET BOTTLE COMPANY			
2	Manufacturing Costs—Budget Performance Report			
3	For the Month Ended March, 31, 2012			
4		Actual Costs	Standard Cost at Actual Volume (500,000 bottles)	Cost Variance— (Favorable) Unfavorable
5				
6				
7				
8				
9				
10				
11				
12				
13				
14				

c.

EXERCISE 23-4

a.

Price variance:

Quantity variance:

Total direct materials cost variance:

b.

EXERCISE 23-5

Price variance:

_____
_____
_____
_____
_____

Quantity variance:

_____
_____
_____
_____
_____

Total direct materials cost variance:

_____
_____
_____
_____
_____

EXERCISE 23-6

_____
_____
_____
_____
_____
_____
_____
_____
_____

EXERCISE 23-7

a.

b.

EXERCISE 23-8

a.

Rate variance:

Time variance:

Total direct labor cost variance:

b.

EXERCISE 23-9

a. Rate variance:

Time variance:

Total direct labor cost variance:

b. Debit to Work in Process:

EXERCISE 23-10

a.

(1) Cutting Department

Rate variance:

Time variance:

Total direct labor cost variance:

(2) Sewing Department

Rate variance:

Time variance:

EXERCISE 23-10, Concluded

Total direct labor cost variance:

b.

EXERCISE 23-11

a.

b.

EXERCISE 23-11, Concluded

c.

EXERCISE 23-12

a.

EXERCISE 23-12, Concluded

b.

EXERCISE 23-13

Step 1:

Name _____

EXERCISE 23-13, Concluded

Step 2:

Step 3:

EXERCISE 23-14

	A	B	C	D
1	WESTERN WOOD PRODUCTS COMPANY			
2	Factory Overhead Cost Budget—Press Department			
3	For the Month Ended March 31, 2010			
4				
5				
6				
7				
8				
9				
10				
11				
12				
13				
14				
15				
16				
17				
18				

EXERCISE 23-15

a.

	A	B	C	D
1	VAN DYCK COMPANY			
2	Monthly Factory Overhead Cost Budget—Fabrication Department			
3				
4				
5				
6				
7				

b. Overhead applied to actual production:

EXERCISE 23-16

Variable factory overhead controllable variance:

Fixed factory overhead volume variance:

Total factory overhead cost variance:

Alternative Computation of Overhead Variances:

EXERCISE 23-17

a. Controllable variance:

b. Volume variance:

Total factory overhead cost variance:

Alternative Computation of Overhead Variances:

EXERCISE 23-18

Correct Determination of Factory Overhead Cost Variances:

Alternative Computation of Overhead Variances:

EXERCISE 23-19

MEDICAL MOLDED PRODUCTS INC.
Factory Overhead Cost Variance Report—Trim Department
For the Month Ended March 31, 2012

	Budget (at actual production)	Actual	Variances — Favorable	Unfavorable
Productive capacity for the month				
Actual productive capacity used for the month				

EXERCISE 23-19, Concluded

Alternative Computation of Overhead Variances:

EXERCISE 23-20

a. and b.

JOURNAL

	DATE	DESCRIPTION	POST. REF.	DEBIT	CREDIT
1					
2					
3					
4					
5					
6					
7					
8					

Name _____ Chapter 23

EXERCISE 23-21

JOURNAL PAGE

	DATE	DESCRIPTION	POST. REF.	DEBIT	CREDIT	
1						1
2						2
3						3
4						4
5						5
6						6
7						7
8						8

EXERCISE 23-22

Income Statement

	FAVORABLE	UNFAVORABLE	

EXERCISE 23-23

a. and b.

	Input Measure	Output Measure	Explanation
Average computer response time to customer "clicks"			
Dollar amount of returned goods			
Elapsed time between customer order and product delivery			
Maintenance dollars divided by hardware investment			
Number of customer complaints divided by the number of orders			
Number of misfilled orders divided by number of orders			
Number of orders per warehouse employee			
Number of page faults or errors due to software programming errors			
Number of software fixes per week			
Server (computer) downtime			
Training dollars per programmer			

EXERCISE 23-24

a. Input Measures:

Output Measures:

b.

This Page Not Used.

PROBLEM 23-1 ___

a.

b. <u>**Direct Materials Cost Variance**</u>

Price variance:

_____

_____

_____

_____

Quantity variance:

_____

_____

_____

_____

Total direct materials cost variance:

_____

_____

_____

_____

894 Name _____ Chapter 23

PROBLEM 23-1 ___, Concluded

c. **Direct Labor Cost Variance**

Rate variance:

_____
_____
_____
_____
_____
_____

Time variance:

_____
_____
_____
_____
_____
_____

Total direct labor cost variance:

_____
_____
_____
_____
_____
_____

PROBLEM 23-2 ___

1. a.

			TOTAL

PROBLEM 23-2 ___, Concluded

b.

			TOTAL

2.

PROBLEM 23-3 ___

a. **Direct Materials Cost Variance**

Price variance:

_____
_____
_____
_____

Quantity variance:

_____
_____
_____
_____

Total direct materials cost variance:

_____
_____
_____
_____

b. **Direct Labor Cost Variance**

Rate variance:

_____
_____
_____
_____

Time variance:

_____
_____
_____
_____

Total direct labor cost variance:

_____
_____
_____
_____

PROBLEM 23-3 ___, Concluded

c.

Factory Overhead Cost Variance

Alternative Computation of Overhead Variances:

PROBLEM 23-4 ___

	A	B	C	D	E
1					
2	Factory Overhead Cost Variance Report—_____ Department				
3					
4	Normal capacity for the month				
5	Actual production for the month				
6					
7				Variances	
8		Budget	Actual	Favorable	Unfavorable
9					
10					
11					
12					
13					
14					
15					
16					
17					
18					
19					
20					
21					
22					
23					
24					
25					
26					
27					
28					

PROBLEM 23-4 ___, Concluded

Alternative Computation of Overhead Variances:

PROBLEM 23-5 ___

1.

2.

3.

4.

PROBLEM 23-5 ___, Concluded

5.

6.

COMPREHENSIVE PROBLEM 5

Part A

1.

2.

3.

4.

COMPREHENSIVE PROBLEM 5, Continued
Part B

5.

Production Budget

	CASES

6.

Direct Materials Purchases Budget

	CREAM BASE (OZS.)	NATURAL OILS (OZS.)	BOTTLES (BOTTLES)	TOTAL

COMPREHENSIVE PROBLEM 5, Continued

7.

Direct Labor Budget

	MIXING	FILLING	TOTAL

8.

Factory Overhead Budget

COMPREHENSIVE PROBLEM 5, Continued

9.

Budgeted Income Statement

COMPREHENSIVE PROBLEM 5, Continued
Part C

10.

Direct Materials Price Variance:

	CREAM BASE	NATURAL OILS	BOTTLES

Direct Materials Quantity Variance:

	CREAM BASE	NATURAL OILS	BOTTLES

COMPREHENSIVE PROBLEM 5, Continued

11.

Direct Labor Rate Variance:

	MIXING DEPARTMENT	FILLING DEPARTMENT

Direct Labor Time Variance:

	MIXING DEPARTMENT	FILLING DEPARTMENT

COMPREHENSIVE PROBLEM 5, Continued

12.

Factory Overhead Controllable Variance:

13.

Factory Overhead Volume Variance:

COMPREHENSIVE PROBLEM 5, Concluded

Alternative Computation of Overhead Variances:

14.

EXERCISE 24-1

a.

Gehring Company
Budget Performance Report—Vice-President, Production
For the Month Ended April 30, 2012

Plant	Budget	Actual	Over Budget	Under Budget
Mid-Atlantic Region	$624,000	$622,500		$1,500
West Region	446,400	444,000		2,400
South Region	(g) _____	(h) _____	(i) $ _____	_____
	(j) $ _____	(k) $ _____	(l) $ _____	$3,900

Gehring Company
Budget Performance Report—Manager, South Region Plant
For the Month Ended April 30, 2012

Department	Budget	Actual	Over Budget	Under Budget
Chip Fabrication	(a) $ _____	(b) $ _____	(c) $ _____	
Electronic Assembly	127,680	129,360	1,680	
Final Assembly	205,500	204,960		$540
	(d) $ _____	(e) $ _____	(f) $ _____	$540

Gehring Company
Budget Performance Report—Supervisor, Chip Fabrication
For the Month Ended April 30, 2012

Department	Budget	Actual	Over Budget	Under Budget
Factory wages	$ 36,960	$ 39,600	$2,640	
Materials	104,400	103,680		$720
Power and light	5,760	6,840	1,080	
Maintenance	10,080	11,040	960	—
	$-157,200	$-161,160	$4,680	$720

b.

_____
_____
_____
_____
_____
_____
_____
_____

EXERCISE 24-1, Concluded

EXERCISE 24-2

Divisional Income Statements

	COMMERCIAL DIVISION	RESIDENTIAL DIVISION

EXERCISE 24-3

a. Electronic data processing: _____

b. Central purchasing: _____

c. Accounts receivable: _____

d. Legal: _____

e. Duplication services: _____

f. Telecommunications: _____

Name _____   **Chapter 24** 913

EXERCISE 24-4

a. Telecommunications: _____

b. Accounts Receivable: _____

c. Central Purchasing: _____

d. Training: _____

e. Computer Support: _____

f. Conferences: _____

g. Employee Travel: _____

h. Payroll Accounting: _____

EXERCISE 24-5

a.

	RESIDENTIAL	COMMERCIAL	GOVERNMENT CONTRACT	TOTAL

b.

_____
_____
_____
_____
_____

	RESIDENTIAL	COMMERCIAL	GOVERNMENT CONTRACT	TOTAL

_____
_____
_____
_____

EXERCISE 24-5, Concluded

c.
_____
_____
_____
_____
_____
_____
_____
_____
_____

EXERCISE 24-6

a. Help desk: _____
_____

Network center: _____
_____

Electronic mail: _____
_____

Local voice support: _____
_____

b. Help desk: _____
_____

Network center: _____
_____

Electronic mail: _____
_____

Local voice support: _____
_____

EXERCISE 24-7

	Divisional Income Statements			
	WHOLESALE DIVISION		RETAIL DIVISION	

Supporting calculations:

EXERCISE 24-8

a.

b.

Divisional Income Statements

	PASSENGER DIVISION		CARGO DIVISION	

Supporting calculations:

EXERCISE 24-9

Divisional Income Statements

	WINTER SPORTS DIVISION	SUMMER SPORTS DIVISION

Supporting Schedule:
Service Department Charges

	WINTER SPORTS DIVISION	SUMMER SPORTS DIVISION	TOTAL

EXERCISE 24-10

a. Retail Division: _____

   Commercial Division: _____

   Internet Division: _____

b. _____

EXERCISE 24-11

a.

	RETAIL DIVISION	COMMERCIAL DIVISION	INTERNET DIVISION

b.

_____

EXERCISE 24-12

Rate of Return on Investment	=	Profit Margin	×	Investment Turnover
10%	=	8%	×	(a) _____
(b) _____	=	15%	×	0.80
14%	=	(c) _____	×	2.00
20%	=	16%	×	(d) _____
(e) _____	=	10%	×	1.50

EXERCISE 24-13

a.

b.

EXERCISE 24-14

a. _____

Media Networks: _____

Parks and Resorts: _____

Studio Entertainment: _____

Consumer Products: _____

b. _____

EXERCISE 24-15

Invested Assets	Income from Operations	Rate of Return on Investment	Minimum Rate of Return	Minimum Acceptable Income from Operations	Residual Income
$920,000	$202,400	(a) _____	15%	(b) _____	(c) _____
$610,000	(d) _____	(e) _____	(f) _____	$67,100	$24,400
$440,000	(g) _____	16%	(h) _____	$57,200	(i) _____
$280,000	$50,400	(j) _____	14%	(k) _____	(l) _____

Calculations:

(a) _____ (g) _____
(b) _____ (h) _____
(c) _____ (i) _____
(d) _____ (j) _____
(e) _____ (k) _____
(f) _____ (l) _____

EXERCISE 24-16

a.

	Sales	Income from Operations	Invested Assets	Rate of Return on Investment	Profit Margin	Investment Turnover
North	$625,000	(a) _____	(b) _____	20%	10%	(c) _____
South	(d) _____	$84,000	(e) _____	(f) _____	14%	1.-5
East	$800,000	(g) _____	$320,000	18%	(h) _____	(i) _____
West	$950,000	$142,500	$950,000	(j) _____	(k) _____	(l) _____

Calculations:

(a) _____ (g) _____
(b) _____ (h) _____
(c) _____ (i) _____
(d) _____ (j) _____
(e) _____ (k) _____
(f) _____ (l) _____

b. North Division: _____

   South Division: _____

   East Division: _____

   West Division: _____

c. (1) _____

   (2) _____

   _____

   _____

   _____

EXERCISE 24-17

a. _____

Hotel Ownership: _____

Vacation Ownership: _____

b.

	HOTEL OWNERSHIP	VACATION OWNERSHIP

c.

Name _____   **Chapter 24 923**

EXERCISE 24-18

Average cardmember spending: _____
_____
_____

Cards in force: _____
_____
_____

Earnings growth: _____
_____
_____

Hours of credit consultant training: _____
_____
_____

Investment in information technology: _____
_____
_____

Number of Internet features: _____
_____
_____

Number of merchant signings: _____
_____
_____

Number of card choices: _____
_____
_____

Number of new card launches: _____
_____
_____

Return on equity: _____
_____
_____

Revenue growth: _____
_____
_____

EXERCISE 24-19

a.

b.

EXERCISE 24-20

a.

b.

c.

EXERCISE 24-21

a.

EXERCISE 24-21, Concluded

b.

c.

d.

PROBLEM 24-1 ___

1.

Budget Performance Report — _____

	BUDGET	ACTUAL	OVER BUDGET	UNDER BUDGET

2.

This Page Not Used.

PROBLEM 24-2 ___

1.

Divisional Income Statements

Supporting schedules:

PROBLEM 24-2 ___, Concluded

2.

3.

PROBLEM 24-3 ___

1.

Divisional Income Statements

2.

PROBLEM 24-3 ___, Concluded

3.

PROBLEM 24-4 ___

1.

2.

Estimated Income Statements

	PROPOSAL 1	PROPOSAL 2	PROPOSAL 3

PROBLEM 24-4 ___, Concluded

3.

4.

5.

PROBLEM 24-5 ___

1.

Divisional Income Statements

2.

PROBLEM 24-5 ___, Concluded

3.

4.

PROBLEM 24-6 ___

1.

2.

PROBLEM 24-6 ___, Continued

3.

Divisional Income Statements

			TOTAL

PROBLEM 24-6 ___, Continued

4.

PROBLEM 24-6 ___, Concluded

5. a. and b.

EXERCISE 25-1

a.

Proposal to Lease or Sell Machinery

b. _____

EXERCISE 25-2

Proposal to Lease or Buy Machinery

Name _____

EXERCISE 25-3

a.

Proposal to Continue or Discontinue King Cola

b. _____

EXERCISE 25-4

a.

Continue Cups or Discontinue Cups

	CONTINUE CUPS	DISCONTINUE CUPS	DIFFERENTIAL EFFECT ON INCOME

b. _____

EXERCISE 25-5

a.

EXERCISE 25-5, Concluded

b. _____

c.

	INVESTOR SERVICES (IN MILLIONS)	INSTITUTIONAL SERVICES (IN MILLIONS)

d. _____

EXERCISE 25-6

EXERCISE 25-7

a.

Proposal to Make or Buy Carrying Case

b.

EXERCISE 25-8

a.

Proposal to Layout Pages Internally or Purchase Page Layout Services

b.

c.

EXERCISE 25-9

a. *Proposal to Continue with or Replace Old Machine*

b.

EXERCISE 25-10

a.

Proposal to Continue with or Replace Old Machine

b. _____

c. _____

EXERCISE 25-11

EXERCISE 25-12

a.

Proposal to Process Columbian Coffee Further

b.

c.

EXERCISE 25-12, Concluded

EXERCISE 25-13

a.

b.

c.

EXERCISE 25-14

EXERCISE 25-15

a.

b.

EXERCISE 25-16

a. _____
b. _____
c. _____

d.

EXERCISE 25-17

a. _____
b. _____
c. _____

d.

EXERCISE 25-18

a.

b.

Name _____

EXERCISE 25-19

a. _____

b. _____

c.

EXERCISE 25-20

	TYPE 5	TYPE 10	TYPE 20

Calculations:

EXERCISE 25-20, Concluded

EXERCISE 25-21

a.

	LARGE	MEDIUM	SMALL	TOTAL

b. _____

	LARGE	MEDIUM	SMALL

EXERCISE 25-22

EXERCISE 25-23

	STATIONARY BICYCLE		
	TREADMILL		

EXERCISE 25-24

a.

b.

	CUSTOM		STANDARD	

EXERCISE 25-24, Concluded

c.

d.

EXERCISE 25-25

a.

Name _____

EXERCISE 25-25, Concluded

b. _____

APPENDIX EXERCISE 25-26

a.

b. _____

Name _____

APPENDIX EXERCISE 25-26, Concluded

c.

APPENDIX EXERCISE 25-27

a. _____

b. _____

c. _____

This Page Not Used.

PROBLEM 25-1 ___

1.

_____ *Proposal to* _____

2.

_____

_____

PROBLEM 25-1 ___, Concluded

3.

PROBLEM 25-2 ___

1.

Proposal to Continue with or Replace Old Machine

2.

This Page Not Used.

PROBLEM 25-3 ___

1.

Proposals for Sales Promotion Campaign

2.

This Page Not Used.

PROBLEM 25-4 ___

1.

_____ _Proposal to Process_ _____ _Further_ _____

2.

This Page Not Used.

PROBLEM 25-5 ___

1. _____

2. a.

b. _____

c.

3. (APPENDIX) a.

b. _____

PROBLEM 25-5 ___, Concluded

c.

4. (APPENDIX)

a. _____

b. _____

c.

5. _____

6. a.

Proposal to Reject or Accept Order _____

b. _____

PROBLEM 25-6 ___

1.

2.

Explanation:

PROBLEM 25-6 ___, Concluded

3.

PROBLEM 25-7 ___

1.

2.

PROBLEM 25-7 ___, Concluded

3.

EXERCISE 26-1

	TESTING EQUIPMENT	VEHICLE

EXERCISE 26-2

EXERCISE 26-3

EXERCISE 26-4

	YEAR 1	YEARS 2-9	LAST YEAR

EXERCISE 26-5

	NET CASH FLOW	CUMULATIVE NET CASH FLOWS

EXERCISE 26-6

a.

	LIQUID SOAP		BODY LOTION	
	NET CASH FLOW	CUMULATIVE NET CASH FLOWS	NET CASH FLOW	CUMULATIVE NET CASH FLOWS

b.

Name _____   Chapter 26

EXERCISE 26-7

a.

Year	Present Value of $1 at 15%	Net Cash Flow	Present Value of Net Cash Flow
1			
2			
3			
4			
Total			
Amount to be invested			
Net present value			

b. _____

_____

EXERCISE 26-8

a. Cash Flows:

	2012	2013	2014	2015	2016

b.

Year	Net Cash Flow [from part (a).]	Present Value of $1 at 12%	Present Value of Net Cash Flow
2012			
2013			
2014			
2015			
2016			
Total present value of cash flows			
Investment in delivery truck			
Net present value of delivery truck			

EXERCISE 26-8, Concluded

c. _____

_____

_____

_____

EXERCISE 26-9

a.

	(IN MILLIONS)	

b.

	(IN MILLIONS, EXCEPT PRESENT VALUE FACTOR)

c. _____

_____

_____

_____

EXERCISE 26-10

a.

b.

c.

d.

EXERCISE 26-11

a.

b.

EXERCISE 26-12

a.

b.

EXERCISE 26-13

a. _____

Sewing Machine:

Packing Machine:

b.

c. _____

EXERCISE 26-14

a.

b.

c.

EXERCISE 26-15

a.

b.

c.

EXERCISE 26-15, Concluded

EXERCISE 26-16

a.

b.

EXERCISE 26-17

a.

b.

EXERCISE 26-18

a. Delivery Truck:

Bagging Machine:

b.

EXERCISE 26-19

a.

b.

c.

EXERCISE 26-20

EXERCISE 26-21

Processing Mill:

Year	Present Value of $1 at 15%	Net Cash Flow	Present Value of Net Cash Flow
1			
2			
3			
4			
4			
Total			
Amount to be invested			
Net present value			

Electric Shovel:

Year	Present Value of $1 at 15%	Net Cash Flow	Present Value of Net Cash Flow
1			
2			
3			
4			
Total			
Amount to be invested			
Net present value			

Conclusion with explanation:

_____
_____
_____
_____
_____
_____
_____

EXERCISE 26-22

a.

Blending Equipment:

Computer System:

b.

PROBLEM 26-1 ___

1. a. _____

_____

_____

_____

_____

b.

Year	Present Value of $1 at ____%	Net Cash Flow		Present Value of Net Cash Flow	
		Project _____	Project _____	Project _____	Project _____
1					
2					
3					
4					
5					
Total					
Amount to be invested					
Net present value					

2.

_____

_____

_____

_____

_____

_____

_____

_____

_____

This Page Not Used.

PROBLEM 26-2 ___

1. a.

Year	Net Cash Flow	Cumulative Net Cash Flow

Year	Net Cash Flow	Cumulative Net Cash Flow

b.

Year	Present Value of $1 at ____%	Net Cash Flow		Present Value of Net Cash Flow	
1					
2					
3					
4					
5					
Total					
Amount to be invested					
Net present value					

2.

_____
_____
_____
_____
_____
_____
_____
_____
_____
_____
_____
_____

This Page Not Used.

Name _____   Chapter 26   995

PROBLEM 26-3 ___

1. Proposal (Project) _____:

Year	Present Value of $1 at ____%	Net Cash Flow	Present Value of Net Cash Flow
1			
2			
3			
Total..			
Amount to be invested..			
Net present value			

Proposal (Project) _____:

Year	Present Value of $1 at ____%	Net Cash Flow	Present Value of Net Cash Flow
1			
2			
3			
Total..			
Amount to be invested..			
Net present value			

Proposal (Project) _____:

Year	Present Value of $1 at ____%	Net Cash Flow	Present Value of Net Cash Flow
1			
2			
3			
Total..			
Amount to be invested..			
Net present value			

PROBLEM 26-3 ___, Concluded

2.

3.

PROBLEM 26-4 ___

1. a.

Project: _____

Project: _____

b. _____

PROBLEM 26-4 ___, Concluded

2. a. and b.

3.

PROBLEM 26-5 ___

1. Net present value analysis:

_____

_____

2. Net present value analysis:

Year	Present Value of $1 at ___%	Net Cash Flow		Present Value of Net Cash Flow	
		Site _____	Site _____	Site _____	Site _____
1					
2					
3					
4					
4					
Total					
Amount to be invested					
Net present value					

PROBLEM 26-5 ___, Concluded

3.

PROBLEM 26-6 ___

1.

Proposal A:

Year	Net Cash Flow	Cumulative Net Cash Flows

_____
_____
_____

Proposal B:

Year	Net Cash Flow	Cumulative Net Cash Flows

_____
_____
_____

Proposal C:

Year	Net Cash Flow	Cumulative Net Cash Flows

_____
_____
_____

PROBLEM 26-6 ___, Continued

Proposal D:

Year	Net Cash Flow	Cumulative Net Cash Flows

_____
_____
_____

2.

Proposal A: _____
_____
_____
_____

Proposal B: _____
_____
_____
_____

Proposal C: _____
_____
_____
_____

Proposal D: _____
_____
_____
_____

Name _____

PROBLEM 26-6 ___, Continued

3.

Proposal	Cash Payback Period	Average Rate of Return	Accept for Further Analysis	Reject
A				
B				
C				
D				

4. Proposal ___:

Year	Present Value of $1 at ___%	Net Cash Flow	Present Value of Net Cash Flow
1			
2			
3			
4			
5			
Total..			
Amount to be invested..			
Net present value			

PROBLEM 26-6 ___, Concluded

Proposal ___:

Year	Present Value of $1 at ____%	Net Cash Flow	Present Value of Net Cash Flow
1			
2			
3			
4			
5			
Total			
Amount to be invested			
Net present value			

5.

6.

7.

8.